THE TEACHINGS OF

Lorenzo Snow

THE TEACHINGS OF
Lorenzo Snow

Fifth President
of
The Church of Jesus Christ
of Latter-day Saints

Compiled by
Clyde J. Williams

Bookcraft
Salt Lake City, Utah

Lithographed in the United States of America
PUBLISHERS PRESS
Salt Lake City, Utah

Contents

Preface

As a student of the gospel and a teacher in the Church Educational System, I have for many years valued the books which contain the teachings of latter-day prophets. I go to them often for inspiration and direction. As I became acquainted with these writings over the years, it came to my attention that no one had ever published a compilation of the teachings of President Lorenzo Snow. It became my desire to have President Snow's teachings available, as are those of the other latter-day prophets.

Although many of Lorenzo Snow's addresses have not been preserved for us, those which remain provide us with a veritable treasure of gospel insights. In the process of reading and rereading each of President Snow's discourses, I have come to more fully appreciate him as one who was endowed with both wisdom and humility. He was one who consistently sought the companionship of the Spirit.

President Snow was the last prophet to have known and worked with the Prophet Joseph Smith as a mature adult. His experience with the Church spans seven decades—from 1831, when his mother and his sister Leonora joined the Church, to his presidential years at the dawn of the twentieth century. From the day of his baptism in 1836 to his death in 1901, he was a faithful servant of the Lord.

Lorenzo Snow is remembered best for three things. First, he is remembered for his emphasis on tithing, which helped bring the Church out of financial bondage in the last three years of his life. Concerning this period President Heber J. Grant said: "I know that Lorenzo Snow was a prophet of God. . . . [He] came to the presidency of the Church when he was eighty-five years of age, and what he accomplished during the next three years of his life is simply marvelous to contemplate. He lifted the Church from almost financial bankruptcy . . . and made its credit A-number-one; . . . this man, beyond the age of ability in the estimation of the world, this man who had not been engaged in financial affairs, took hold on the finances of the Church of Christ, under the inspiration of the living God, and in those three years changed everything financially from darkness to light. I know that Lorenzo Snow was God's mouthpiece upon the earth, that he was the representative of the Lord, and that he was in very deed a prophet of God.'' (*Improvement Era,* 22:847.)

Second, Lorenzo Snow is remembered for his couplet "As man now is, God once was; as God now is, man may be." These words came by revelation to Lorenzo when he was a young man in Nauvoo. Their truthfulness was reaffirmed when he heard the Prophet Joseph Smith teach the very same concept. Over the years this simple yet profound statement has stirred the minds of many individuals and caused them to further investigate The Church of Jesus Christ of Latter-day Saints.

Third, President Snow is remembered because of his powerful testimony of the Lord Jesus Christ. Shortly after the death of President Wilford Woodruff, President Snow was privileged to see the Savior in the Salt Lake Temple. At his funeral, President Joseph F. Smith expressed the feeling that, with the exception of the Prophet Joseph Smith, he did not believe any man ever stood upon the earth in this generation who bore a stronger, more clear-cut testimony of the Savior and this latter-day work than did President Lorenzo Snow.

I hope that this book will help readers to more fully understand the gospel, and that it will strengthen their conviction that Lorenzo Snow was indeed a prophet of God.

Acknowledgments

I express appreciation to Sandra Burke and Lorna Shaw, who typed the original manuscript, and to my wife, Kathy, who assisted in innumerable ways as the project progressed.

Key to Abbreviations

BLS   Eliza R. Snow Smith, *Biography and Family Record of Lorenzo Snow* (Salt Lake City: Deseret News Company, 1884)

CR   Conference Reports

DN   *Deseret News*

DW   *Deseret Weekly*

IE   *Improvement Era*

JD   *Journal of Discourses,* 26 vols. (London: Latter-day Saints' Book Depot, 1855-86)

JH   Journal History of The Church of Jesus Christ of Latter-day Saints (manuscripts, LDS Church Archives)

MFP   *Messages of the First Presidency,* vol. 3; comp. James R. Clark (Salt Lake City: Bookcraft, 1966)

MS   *Millennial Star*

SML   *Scrapbook of Mormon Literature,* vol. 1; comp. Ben E. Rich (Chicago: Henry C. Etton & Co., 1910?)

Highlights in the Life of Lorenzo Snow

1814   Born April 3 in Mantua, Portage County, Ohio.

1831   His mother and his sister Leonora join the Church.

1835   Enters Oberlin College. His sister Eliza R. joins the Church.

1836   Attends the School of the Prophets in Kirtland; is baptized on June 23 by John Boynton of the Council of the Twelve.

1837   Serves a mission in Ohio.

1838-39   Moves to Far West; serves a mission to southern Missouri, Illinois, Kentucky, and Ohio.

1840-43   Serves a mission to Great Britain; presents a copy of the Book of Mormon to Queen Victoria.

1843   Teaches school at Lima, Illinois.

1844   Learns of the martyrdom of Joseph Smith while on an electioneering mission for the Prophet in Ohio.

1845   Marries Charlotte Squires, Mary Adaline Goodard, Sarah Ann Richards, and Harriet Amelia Squires.

1846-48   Presides over Mt. Pisgah; crosses the plains.

1848   Arrives in the Salt Lake Valley.

1849   Ordained an Apostle by Heber C. Kimball on February 12 at the age of thirty-four; helps organize the Perpetual Emigration Fund.

1849-52   Serves a mission to Italy and Europe.

1852   Organizes the Polysophical Society (an organization for cultural and intellectual development).

1853   Called to preside over the colonizing of Box Elder County.

1854   Participates in the organization of the Philosophical Society—later called the Universal Scientific Society.

1856   Becomes president of Box Elder Stake.

1864   Serves a short-term mission to Hawaii.

1865   Organizes the Brigham City Cooperative
            Association.

1872-82   Serves as president of the Utah Territorial Legislative
            Council.

1872-73   Tours the Holy Land with George A. Smith; partici-
            pates in the rededication of Palestine for the return
            of the Jews.

1873-77   Sustained as one of seven counselors to President
            Brigham Young.

1885   Serves a short-term mission to the Indians in the
            northwestern United States.

1886-87   Serves an eleven-month prison term on a charge of
            plural marriage.

1888   Dedicates the Manti Temple.

1889   Becomes President of the Council of the Twelve at
            seventy-five.

1893   Called as president of the Salt Lake Temple.

1898   Sustained as President of the Church on
            September 13 at eighty-four.

1899   Preaches tithing in St. George, Utah.

1901   Dies in Salt Lake City at eighty-seven.

CHAPTER 1

As God Is, Man May Be

Be as great as you want to be. You who have aspirations to be great—and there is no wrong in that—should realize... the support that you should give to those over you, so that when you are placed in responsible positions you may demand of the Lord the faith and support of the people. You will all be great someday, as great as you want to be. I remember an incident which occurred in Kirtland when I received my first patriarchal blessing from Father Smith. A better man never existed, nor was there a man better-loved than he. I was introduced by my sister Eliza R., though at that time I was not a Latter-day Saint and had no idea of becoming one. He said to me: "Don't worry, take it calmly and the Lord will show you, and you will want to be baptized." He told me another thing that greatly surprised me. He said, "You will be great, and as great as you want to be, as great as God Himself, and you will not wish to be greater." I could not understand this, but years after in Nauvoo while talking upon a principle of the gospel, the Spirit of God rested powerfully upon me and showed me more clearly than I can now see your faces a certain principle and its glory, and it came to me summarized in this brief sentence: "As man is now, God once was; as God is now man may be." The Spirit of God was on me in a marvelous manner all that day, and I stored that great truth away in my mind. I felt that I had learnt something that I ought not to communicate to others. (15 June 1901, DN, p. 1.)

"As God now is, man may be." Now, I have told you what Father Smith said to me, that I should become as great as I could want to be, even as great as God Himself. About two years and a half after, in Nauvoo, I asked Elder Sherwood to explain a certain passage of scripture; and while he was endeavoring to give an explanation, the Spirit of God fell upon me to a marked extent, and the Lord revealed to me, just as plainly as the sun at noonday, this principle, which I put in a couplet: "As man now is, God once was; As God now is, man may be." That fulfilled Father Smith's declaration. Nothing was ever revealed more distinctly than that was to me. Of course, now that it is so well known it may not appear such a wonderful manifestation; but when I received it, the knowledge was marvelous to me. This principle, in substance, is found also in the scriptures. The Lord said to John, as recorded in the third chapter of his Revelation: "To him that overcometh will I grant to sit with me in my throne, even as I also overcame, and am set down with my Father in his throne." (20 July 1901, JH, p. 4.)

We are to govern our eternal posterity. Now I will say what I received in vision, which was just as clear as the sun ever shone. The knowledge that was communicated to me I embraced in this couplet: "As man now is, God once was. As God now is, man may be." That is a very wonderful thing. It was to me. I did not know but that I had come into possession of knowledge that I had no business with; but I knew it was true. Nothing of this kind had ever reached my ears before. It was preached a few years after that; at least, the Prophet Joseph taught this idea to the Twelve Apostles. Now, however, it is common property; but I do not know how many there are here that have got a real knowledge of these things in their hearts. If you have, I will tell you what its effects will be. As John said, "Every man that hath this hope in him purifieth himself, even as [God] is pure" (1 John 3:3).

Now, how is it that God proposes to confer this mighty honor upon us and to raise us to this condition of glory and exaltation? Who are we that God should do all this for us? Why, we are just beginning to find out that we are the offspring of God, born with the same faculties and powers as He possesses, capable of enlargement through the experience that we are now passing through in our second estate. Let me illustrate. Here is an emperor sitting upon his throne, governing and controlling his empire wisely and properly. He has an infant son that sits upon the knee of its mother. That son he proposes to one day set upon his throne, to govern and control his empire. Here is that infant, perfectly helpless, not knowing how to sustain its own life, not able to walk alone, without any knowledge; and here is this mighty emperor sitting upon his throne and governing his vast empire. Who would believe that he could raise that infant up to such a condition as to make it suitable to be placed on his throne? No one would, unless he had seen such things accomplished in his experience; seen the infant develop into boyhood, and then to manhood, possessing all the powers, faculties and possibilities of its father. Now, we are the sons and daughters of God. He has begotten us in His own image. He has given us faculties and powers that are capable of enlargement until His fulness is reached which He has promised—until we shall sit upon thrones, governing and controlling our posterity from eternity to eternity, and increasing eternally. That is the fact in regard to these matters.

God has pointed out the results of traveling upon this road of glory and exaltation, and the promises are sure. The Lord knew precisely what He could do. He knew what materials He had to operate with, and He knew just what He said. If we do the part that He has assigned unto us, and keep our second estate, we shall be sure to realize these promises in every particular, and more than you and I can possibly comprehend. (3 November 1894, DW, 49:610.)

Man can possess the same glory as God. Through a continual course of progression, our Heavenly Father has received exaltation and glory, and He points us out the same path; and inasmuch as He is clothed with power, authority, and glory, He says,

"Walk ye up and come in possession of the same glory and happiness that I possess."

In the gospel, those things have been made manifest unto us; and we are perfectly assured that, inasmuch as we are faithful, we shall eventually come in possession of everything that the mind of man can conceive of—everything that heart can desire. (11 October 1857, JD, 5:313.)

Our spirit birth gave us godlike capabilities. We were born in the image of God our Father; He begot us like unto Himself. There is the nature of deity in the composition of our spiritual organization; in our spiritual birth our Father transmitted to us the capabilities, powers and faculties which He Himself possessed —as much so as the child on its mother's bosom possesses, although in an undeveloped state, the faculties, powers, and susceptibilities of its parent. (14 January 1872, JD, 14:302.)

Free agency is needed for godhood. Now, I believe in the independence of men and women. I believe that men and women have the image of God given them—are formed after the image of God, and possess deity in their nature and character, and that their spiritual organization possesses the qualities and properties of God, and that there is the principle of God in every individual. It is designed that man should act as God, and not be constrained and controlled in everything, but have an independency, an agency and the power to spread abroad and act according to the principle of godliness that is in him, act according to the power and intelligence and enlightenment of God, that he possesses, and not that he should be watched continually, and be controlled, and act as a slave in these matters. (19 October 1879, JD, 20:367.)

Faithful husbands may become gods. I say to you sisters: your husbands, if they are faithful, will be gods in eternity. After we have passed through the various ordeals of life and go to the other life, where our Father dwells, even the God of heaven, the promise is that we shall be like Him. (20 July 1901, JH, p. 4.)

Obedience and purity are requirements of godhood. That exalted position was made manifest to me at a very early day. I had a direct revelation of this. It was most perfect and complete. If there ever was a thing revealed to man perfectly, clearly, so that there could be no doubt or dubiety, this was revealed to me, and it came in these words: "As man now is, God once was; as God now is, man may be." This may appear to some minds as something very strange and remarkable, but it is in perfect harmony with the teachings of Jesus Christ and with His promises. He said: "To him that overcometh will I grant to sit with me in my throne, even as I also overcame, and am set down with my Father in his throne" (Revelation 3:21). The Apostle Paul also taught in this wise: "Let this mind be in you, which was also in Christ Jesus: who being in the form of God, thought it not robbery to be equal with God: but made himself of no reputation, and took upon him the form of a servant, and was made in the likeness of men: and being found in fashion as a man, he humbled himself, and became obedient unto death, even the death of the cross" (Philippians 2:5-8). This is the high destiny of the sons of God, they who overcome, who are obedient to His commandments, who purify themselves even as He is pure. They are to become like Him; they will see Him as He is; they will behold His face and reign with Him in His glory, becoming like unto Him in every particular. (8 October 1898, DW, 57:513.)

We must advance through stages to godhood. As man now is, God once was—even the babe of Bethlehem, advancing to childhood—thence to boyhood, manhood, then to the Godhead. This, then, is the "mark of the prize of man's high calling in Christ Jesus."

We are the offspring of God, begotten by Him in the spirit world, where we partook of His nature as children here partake of the likeness of their parents. Our trials and sufferings give us experience, and establish within us principles of godliness. (10 January 1886, JD, 26:368.)

Our spiritual organism has divinity in itself. I believe that we are the sons and daughters of God, and that He has bestowed upon us the capacity for infinite wisdom and knowledge, because He has given us a portion of Himself. We are told that we were made in His own image, and we find that there is a character of immortality in the soul of man. There is a spiritual organism within this tabernacle, and that spiritual organism has a divinity in itself, though perhaps in an infantile state; but it has within itself the capability of improving and advancing, as the infant that receives sustenance from its mother. Though the infant may be very ignorant, yet there are possibilities in it that by passing through the various ordeals of childhood to maturity enable it to rise to a superiority that is perfectly marvelous, compared with its infantile ignorance. Why and how is it that this is accomplished? Because it possesses the susceptibilities and the capabilities of its father. So in regard to ourselves. There is a divinity within ourselves that is immortal and never dies. Thousands and thousands of years hence we will be ourselves, and nobody else, so far as our individuality is concerned. That never dies from all eternity to all eternity. (10 April 1898, CR, p. 63.)

We are God's offspring. We believe that we are the offspring of our Father in Heaven, and that we possess in our spiritual organizations the same capabilities, powers, and faculties that our Father possesses—although in an infantile state—requiring [us] to pass through a certain course or ordeal by which they will be developed and improved according to the heed we give to the principles we have received. (14 January 1872, JD, 14:300.)

Man can inherit all God possesses. "He that overcometh shall inherit all things" [Revelation 21:7]. What an expression is that? Who believes it? If a father were to say to his son, "My son, be faithful, and follow my counsels, and when you become of age you shall inherit all that I possess," it would mean something, would it not? If the father told the truth, that son would have something to encourage him to be faithful. Did Jesus want to deceive us when He made use of this expression? I will assure you that there is no deception in the language. He meant precisely what He said. (3 November 1894, DW, 49:609.)

We should do good to develop godliness. The idea is not to do good because of the praise of men, but to do good because in doing good we develop godliness within us; and this being the case, we shall become allied to godliness, which will in time become part and portion of our being. (6 May 1882, JD, 23:192.)

Sons of God inherit the Father's throne. The Apostle John says: "Beloved, now are we the sons of God, and it doth not yet appear what we shall be: but we know that, when he shall appear, we shall be like him" (1 John 3:2).

As an illustration, here is an infant upon its mother's breast. It is without power or knowledge to feed and clothe itself. It is so helpless that it has to be fed by its mother. But see its possibilities! This infant has a father and a mother, though it knows scarcely anything about them; and when it gets to be quite a little boy it does not know much about them. Who is its father? Who is its mother? Why, its father is an emperor, its mother is an empress, and they sit upon a throne, governing an empire. This little infant will some day, in all probability, sit upon his father's throne, and govern and control the empire, just as King Edward of England now sits upon the throne of his mother. We should have this in mind; for we are the sons of God, as much so and more, if possible, than we are the sons of our earthly fathers. (20 July 1901, JH, p. 4.)

Women can become like our mother in heaven. You sisters, I suppose, have read that poem which my sister composed years ago, and which is sung quite frequently now in our meetings. It tells us that we not only have a Father in "that high and glorious place," but that we have a Mother too; and you will become as great as your Mother, if you are faithful. (20 July 1901, JH, p. 4.)

Man's destiny is to become like God. "Let this mind be in you, which was also in Christ Jesus: who, being in the form of God, thought it not robbery to be equal with God" (Philippians 2:5-6).

Dear Brother:

> Hast thou not been unwisely bold,
> Man's destiny to thus unfold?
> To raise, promote such high desire,
> Such vast ambition thus inspire?

> Still, 'tis no phantom that we trace
> Man's ultimatum in life's race;
> This royal path has long been trod
> By righteous men, each now a God:

> As Abra'm, Isaac, Jacob, too,
> First babes, then men—to gods they grew.
> As man now is, our God once was;
> As now God is, so man may be,—
> Which doth unfold man's destiny.

> For John declares: When Christ we see
> Like unto him we'll truly be.
> And he who has this hope within,
> Will purify himself from sin.

> Who keep this object grand in view,
> To folly, sin, will bid adieu,
> Nor wallow in the mire anew;

> Nor ever seek to carve his name
> High on the shaft of worldly fame;
> But here his ultimatum trace:
> The head of all his spirit-race.

Ah, well, that taught by you, dear Paul,
Though much amazed, we see it all;
Our Father God, has ope'd our eyes,
We cannot view it otherwise.

The boy, like to his father grown,
Has but attained unto his own;
To grow to sire from state of son,
Is not 'gainst Nature's course to run.

A son of God, like God to be,
Would not be robbing Deity;
And he who has this hope within,
Will purify himself from sin.

You're right, St. John, supremely right:
Whoe'er essays to climb this height,
Will cleanse himself of sin entire—
Or else 'twere needless to aspire.

Lorenzo Snow

(IE, 22:660-61; the poem is dated 11 January 1892.)

CHAPTER 2

The Nature of God

God communicates continually to man. The Lord is a consistent being. He does not require the people to do that which is improper, nor does He expect of them anything unreasonable. He gives us a knowledge of what we shall do, inasmuch as we are willing to sacrifice our lives rather than go contrary to that knowledge. He opens to us the secrets of the celestial kingdom, and He is constantly communicating to us things that we never knew before. This knowledge and intelligence is growing upon us continually. (6 April 1900, CR, p. 3.)

Develop the character traits of godliness. Be upright, just, and merciful, exercising a spirit of nobility and godliness in all your intentions and resolutions—in all your acts and dealings. Cultivate a spirit of charity, be ready to do for others more than you would expect from them if circumstances were reversed. Be ambitious to be great, not in the estimation of the worldly minded, but in the eyes of God, and to be great in this sense: "Love the Lord your God with all your might, mind and strength, and your neighbor as yourself." You must love mankind because they are your brethren, the offspring of God. Pray diligently for this spirit of philanthropy, this expansion of thought and feeling, and for power and ability to labor earnestly in the interest of Messiah's kingdom. (May 1884, BLS, p. 487.)

Man is dependent upon God. Now it is so ordered and so arranged, that we are dependent, in a great measure, one upon another. For instance, take us as a people, we are dependent upon a being that is above us to secure our peace, our happiness, our glory, and exaltation; we are individually dependent upon the exertions of an individual who is above ourselves. (1 March 1857, JD, 4:239.)

A man's mind should be single to the glory of God in everything that he starts to accomplish. We should consider that of ourselves we can do nothing. We are the children of God. We are in darkness, only as God enlightens our understanding. We are powerless, only as God helps us. The work that we have to do here is of that nature that we cannot do it unless we have the assistance of the Almighty. (12 May 1894, DW, 48:638.)

We require supernatural aid. To properly discharge the obligations devolving upon us, we require supernatural aid. The character of the religion that we have espoused demands a certain course of conduct that no other religion that we know of requires of its adherents; and the nature of those demands upon us are such that no person can comply with them, unless by assistance from the Almighty. (19 October 1879, JD, 20:362.)

There is safety in doing the will of God. And now all the Latter-day Saints have to do, all that is required of us to make us perfectly safe under all circumstances of trouble or persecution, is to do the will of God: to be honest, faithful, and to keep ourselves devoted to the principles that we have received; do right one by another; trespass upon no man's rights; live by every word that proceedeth from the mouth of God, and His Holy Spirit will aid and assist us under all circumstances, and we will come out of the midst of it all abundantly blessed in our houses, in our families, in our flocks, in our fields—and in every way God will bless us. He will give us knowledge upon knowledge, intelligence upon intelligence, wisdom upon wisdom. (6 October 1879, JD, 20:332.)

Many forget we are working for God. Here is the great trouble with men of the world, and too much so with the Elders of Israel: we forget that we are working for God; we forget that we are here in order to carry out certain purposes that we have promised the Lord that we would carry out. It is a glorious work that we are engaged in. It is the work of the Almighty, and He has selected the men and the women whom He knows from past experience will carry out His purposes. (12 May 1894, DW, 48:638.)

We need God's help to keep the commandments. In and of ourselves we cannot possibly comply with all the commandments that God has given unto us. Jesus Himself could not without divine aid from His Father accomplish His work. He said on one occasion, "I can of mine own self do nothing: as I hear, I judge: and my judgment is just; because I seek not my own will, but the will of the Father which hath sent me" [John 5:30]. And we, if it was necessary for Him, our Lord, to have divine assistance, will find it all the more important to receive His assistance. (6 April 1898, CR, p. 12.)

The Lord's promises will be fulfilled. When the Lord makes promises, and the conditions of those promises are observed, one need not entertain the slightest doubt that the Lord will do His part and fulfill those promises. This can be relied upon. (12 June 1899, JH, p. 13.)

Jesus Christ grew in knowledge. When Jesus lay in the manger, a helpless infant, He knew not that He was the Son of God, and that formerly He created the earth. When the edict of Herod was issued, He knew nothing of it; He had not power to save Himself; and His father and mother had to take Him and fly into Egypt to preserve Him from the effects of that edict. Well, He grew up to manhood, and during His progress it was revealed unto Him who He was, and for what purpose He was in the world. The glory and power He possessed before He came into the world was made known unto Him. It was not a very pleasurable thing to be placed upon the cross and to suffer the excruciating torture that He bore for hours, in order to accomplish the work for which He had come upon the earth. (5 April 1901, CR, p. 3.)

God tests men in decisions. Moses told the Lord that if He did what He proposed—destroy Israel—the nations around would say that He had undertaken a task that He could not succeed in accomplishing. Well, the Lord changed His mind, so it reads, and did not that which He had intended to do. Now, whether the Lord had a disposition in this matter to try Moses, may be a question; but the distinct understanding with Moses was that if he did not plead with the Lord all Israel would be destroyed. [See Numbers 14:12-21.] (10 April 1898, CR, p. 63.)

The hand of God is manifest in the world. We trace the hand of God, His Spirit, His workings upon and among all classes of people, whether Christian or heathen, that His providences may be carried out, and that His designs, formed before the morning stars sang together or the foundations of the earth were laid, may be ultimately fulfilled. He slackens not His hand, He gives not up His designs nor His purposes; but His work is one eternal round. We trace the hand of the Almighty and we see His Spirit moving in all communities for their good, restraining and encouraging, establishing governments and nations, inspiring men to take a course that shall most advance His purposes until the set time shall come when He shall work more fully and effectually for the accomplishment of His designs, and when sorrow, wickedness, evil, crime, bitter disappointments, vexation, distress, and poverty shall cease and be no more known, and the salvation and happiness of His children be secured, when the earth shall be rolled back into its pristine purity and the inhabitants thereof dwell upon it in perfect peace and happiness. (14 January 1872, JD, 14:301.)

God loves and watches over us. There is something grand in the consideration of the fact that the Lord loves us with a most ardent love. The love that a woman exercises toward her offspring cannot equal the love that God exercises toward us. He never leaves us. He is always before us, and upon our right hand and our left hand. Continually He watches over us. (6 October 1898, CR, p. 2.)

CHAPTER 3

The Gospel and Its Principles

A restoration was necessary. It is very evident that the authority of administering in gospel ordinances has been lost for many centuries; for no man can have this authority, except he receive it by direct revelation—either by the voice of God, as Moses did, or by the ministering of angels, as John the Baptist received his message, or by the gift of prophecy, as Paul and Barnabas received theirs (Acts 13:2). Now, it is plain that men have denied immediate revelation for many hundred years past, consequently have not received it, and therefore could not have been sent of God to administer in the fulness of the gospel. God never sends a man on business, except He reveal Himself to that man—never sends a man with a message, in other words, unless He reveal that message to him in a direct manner. The church established by the Apostles gradually fell away, wandered into the wilderness, and lost her authority (her priesthood), and, departing from the order of God, she lost, also, her gifts and graces; she transgressed the laws, and changed the ordinances of the gospel; changed immersion into sprinkling, and quite neglected laying on of hands; despised prophecy, and disbelieved in signs following (Revelation 12:6; Isaiah 25:5). In consequence of this, the Gentiles have been cut off from the fulness of gospel privileges, as Paul said to them in Romans 11:22: "If thou continue in his goodness: otherwise thou also shalt be cut off." (1841, SML, p. 86.)

Mormonism has modified Christianity. The influence of
Mormonism upon religious thought in general is a noteworthy
feature of its career. The preaching and publishing of its
doctrines has had a marked effect in molding and modifying
Christian views and sentiments, and in changing the creeds of the
churches. Infant damnation and the never-ending torture of the
soul (doctrines controverted by Mormonism) are not insisted
upon by the sects as emphatically as they once were, and the
"larger hope" of repentance beyond the grave—an "out-and-
out" Mormon doctrine—is gradually coming to the front in the
reformed conceptions of orthodox Christianity. Other points of
modification are those touching the antiquity of the gospel, and
progress in lieu of stagnation in the life to come. Since a Mormon
poetess wrote a hymn invocation to the Eternal Father and
Mother, it has dawned upon many Christian minds as a reason-
able proposition that we have a Mother as well as a Father in
Heaven. In divers other ways, clearly discernible to the close
student of history, Mormonism has acted as a leaven upon other
religious faiths. Consciously or unconsciously they have absorbed
and utilized it. This is especially manifest in the growth of liberal
ideas among the Protestant churches within the last half century.
(2 January 1902, MS, 64:22.)

The true gospel requires works. When the gospel dispensation
was introduced, gifts and blessings were obtained upon similar
principles—that is, upon obedience to certain established rules.
The Lord still marked out certain acts, promising to all those who
would do them certain peculiar privileges; and when those acts
were performed—observed in every particular—then the blessings promised were sure to be realized. Some vainly imagine that,
under the gospel dispensation, gifts and blessings are obtained
not by external observances, or external works, but merely
through faith and repentance, through mental operations, inde-
pendent of physical. But, laying aside the traditions, super-
stitions, and creeds of men, we will look to the word of God,
where we shall discover that external works, or outward ordi-

nances, under the gospel dispensation, were inseparably connected with inward works, such as faith and repentance. In proof of this, I introduce the following observations: The Savior says, "Why call ye me, Lord, Lord, and do not the things which I say?" Again, He says, "He that heareth my words, and doeth them shall be likened unto a man that built his house upon a rock." And, "He that believeth and is baptized shall be saved." Likewise, He says, "Except a man be born of water and of the Spirit, he cannot enter into the kingdom of God" (John 3:5). These sayings of our Savior require men to perform external works in order to receive their salvation. (1841, SML, p. 78.)

The gospel is no human contrivance. But in the provisions of the gospel which was offered to us, there were fairness and safety; it proposed to give us, through obedience to its requirements, a perfect knowledge of its divine authenticity, so that in leaving our kindred, breaking up our social relations, and going forth from our native land, we should first become perfectly assured that it was no human contrivance, something gotten up to effect some political purpose, or satisfy some worldly ambition, to achieve some private end through human cunning and craftiness. The gospel was plain and simple in its requirements; and there would be no mistaking the precise nature and character of its blessings and promises, nor the manner and time in which they were to be reached. (23 January 1870, JD, 13:285.)

The religion we have received is not a chimera. It is not something that has been devised by the cunning of man, but it is something that has been revealed by the Almighty. It is a fact. It is something that truly exists. It is something that is tangible. It is something that can be laid hold of by the minds of the Latter-day Saints. It is something that can be directly understood, and be fully comprehended, so that there can be no doubt in the mind of any Latter-day Saint in regard to the nature and character of the ultimate outcome of the course that he proposes to pursue in complying with the demands of the gospel he has received. But those demands are of a nature that perhaps would be almost appalling to the minds of individuals that were darkened, that had no light or understanding in regard to the outcome that is expected to be experienced by the Latter-day Saints, inasmuch as they continue faithful in adhering to the principles which they have espoused. (19 October 1879, JD, 20:362-63.)

Religion must better man's condition. A religious system is of but little account when it possesses no virtue nor power to better the condition of people spiritually, intellectually, morally, and physically. Enoch's order of the gospel did for his people all this, and it has done the same in every instance when preached in its purity, and obeyed in sincerity. (6 March 1886, JD, 26:371.)

The gospel brings us closer to God. The Lord wishes to establish a closer and more intimate relationship between Himself and us; He wishes to elevate us in the scale of being and intelligence, and this can only be done through the medium of the everlasting gospel which is specially prepared for this purpose. (6 May 1882, JD, 23:193.)

The gospel today is the same as in ancient times. But when Noah stood up before the people, he preached to them the everlasting gospel. He preached the same gospel that Adam preached. He preached the same gospel that the people of old preached. He preached the same gospel the Apostles preached. He preached the same gospel that we preach, through which a knowledge from God could be obtained as to its truth. (5 October 1882, JD, 23:291.)

The restored gospel conforms to the scriptures. When this gospel or order of things which we have received was presented to us, we carefully compared it with the gospel recorded in the scriptures, and found it alike precisely in every particular, as regarded its forms, ordinances and the authority to administer them, its promise of the Holy Ghost and of the signs that should follow, together with a promise of a knowledge of its divinity. (23 January 1870, JD, 13:288.)

The restored gospel is worth any sacrifice. While we are here studying the interests of Zion, of the honest in heart among the nations of the earth—how we can gather them together, that the fetters under which they are now laboring may be broken—while we are doing this, on the other hand our enemies are scheming for the destruction of these righteous principles, for the purpose of binding the yoke more strongly upon our neck, of destroying those pure and holy principles that have been revealed for the salvation of the honest in heart: principles that are calculated to exalt, to happify, and glorify.

Such principles have been revealed, such principles have been restored, such principles have been held forth by the Elders among the nations as you heard yesterday. For these principles this people have been driven several times; they have forsaken their homes; they have forsaken their enjoyments and the privileges they might have had among the nations; and they would now willingly burn up their dwellings, if they were so commanded. (7 October 1857, JD, 5:322-23.)

The gospel makes us wise. Men may be very good, and yet they may not be very wise, nor so useful as they might be; but the gospel is given to make us wise, and to enable us to get those things in our minds that are calculated to make us happy. (7 April 1861, JD, 9:22.)

Conforming to the gospel brings blessings. I say, with propriety and consistency, that whenever a man will lay aside his prejudice, sectarian notions, and false traditions, and conform to the whole order of the gospel of Jesus Christ, then there is nothing beneath the celestial worlds that can prevent his claiming and receiving the gift of the Holy Ghost and all the blessings connected with the gospel in the apostolic age. (1841, SML, p. 85.)

Baptism is an essential principle. Some deem it wrong to number baptism among the essential principles ordained of God, to be attended to in obtaining remission of sins. In reply, we say that the Savior and Apostles have done so before us, therefore we feel obligated to follow their example. The destruction of the antediluvian world by water was typical of receiving remission of sins through baptism. The earth had become clothed with sin as with a garment; the righteous were brought and saved from the world of sin, even by water; the like figure, even baptism, doth now save us, says Peter (1 Peter 3:21), by the answer of "a good conscience toward God." Noah and his family were removed, and disconnected from sins and pollutions, by means of water; so baptism, the like figure, doth now remove our souls from sins and pollutions, through faith on the great Atonement made upon Calvary. (1841, SML, p. 79.)

Only one mode of baptism is taught in the scriptures. We will now occupy a moment in endeavoring to obtain a proper view of the mode in which baptism was administered. It is quite evident that there was but one way or mode in which this ordinance was to be administered, and that mode was explained to the Apostles, and strictly adhered to in all their administrations. Paul, in writing to the Saints, gives us a plain testimony in favour of immersion (Colossians 2:12; Romans 6:4). That Apostle states there that the Saints had been buried with Christ by baptism.

It is plainly evident they could not have been buried by baptism without having been entirely overwhelmed or covered in water. An object cannot be said to be buried when any portion of it remains uncovered; so, also, a man is not buried in water by baptism unless his whole person is put into the watery element. This explanation of the Apostle upon the mode of baptism very beautifully corresponds with that given by our Savior: "Except ye be born of water." To be born of a thing signifies being placed in that thing, and emerging or coming forth from it; to be born of water must also signify being placed in the womb of waters, and being brought forth again. (1841, SML, pp. 82-83.)

Baptism brings blessings. Baptism in water forming a part of the gospel of Christ, we notice therefore that the servants of God, in early ages, were very particular in attending to its administration; also, it is evident that unless peculiar blessings actually were experienced through baptism, they would have neglected enforcing its observance. If, as some suppose, that faith, repentance, and prayer answer the purpose, in receiving the fulness of gospel privileges, then it is very evident that baptism was a vain and useless work, and had no need to be observed. Naaman would have been performing a vain and foolish work when washing seven times in Jordan's waters, had it been in his power to have been recovered from his affliction merely through faith, repentance, and prayer. Also, Noah and his family were very foolish in performing an external work, in building an ark, provided they could have obtained the same blessing through faith, repentance, and prayer. Furthermore, the Israelites, could they have obtained forgiveness of sins through faith, repentance, and prayer, it would have been folly in them to offer up animals for that purpose. So also under the gospel dispensation, the three thousand people on the day of Pentecost, who were baptized in one day, were very unwise and foolish in submitting to the trouble of baptism, provided the same blessings could have been realized by exercising only faith, repentance, and prayer. (1841, SML, p. 81.)

The blessings of the gospel are not fully comprehended. I presume to say that we do not all of us fully comprehend the blessings and privileges that are prepared in the gospel for us to receive. We do not fully comprehend and we do not have before our view the things which await us in the eternal worlds, nor, indeed, the things which await us in this life and that are calculated to promote our peace and happiness and to answer the desires of our hearts. . . .

Where is the man that will turn aside and throw away those prospects that are embraced in the gospel which we have received? In it there is satisfaction, there is joy, there is stability, there is something upon which to rest our feet, there is a sure foundation to build upon, and upon which to yield that which is required of us. (11 October 1857, JD, 5:312, 314.)

The gospel unifies its followers. The gospel binds together the hearts of all its adherents; it makes no difference, it knows no difference between the rich and the poor; we are all bound as one individual to perform the duties which devolve upon us. (31 January 1877, DN, 25:834.)

The gospel teaches all necessary things. The gospel tells us how to be great, good, and happy. The Spirit of the gospel of Christ teaches all things that are necessary for our present and future welfare. (7 April 1861, JD, 9:21.)

The gospel has been shown by revelation. This scheme of life, this gospel as proclaimed by Joseph Smith, has been shown to us by the revelations of the Almighty, that it is undeniably His will, His word, and His message; not only this, but we find within ourselves a fixed purpose, an unalterable resolution to do, if need be, what many of us have already done—show the sincerity of our convictions of these solemn truths through sacrificing all we possess, not even holding our lives as dear to us as this religion. (23 January 1870, JD, 13:286.)

We have received a gospel of persecution and sacrifice. The gospel that we have received from the beginning is a gospel of persecution and a gospel of sacrifices. It is a gospel and work that requires the utmost diligence in order that we may receive that power, that faith, and that intelligence from the Almighty to such an extent that we may be fully prepared to cope with all the difficulties that may beset our path. (18 April 1887, MS, 49:244-45.)

An important item which was put forward prominently wherever this gospel was announced was that its followers should have abundance of persecutions, and would probably, in the progress of their new life, be compelled to make the most serious sacrifices of wife, children, houses and lands, spoiling of goods, and even life itself, perhaps. No persons are properly prepared to enter upon this new life until they have formed within themselves this resolution. (23 January 1870, JD, 13:290.)

Laying aside the gospel is dangerous. Nothing can be more foolish than the idea of a man laying off his religion like a cloak or garment. There is no such thing as a man laying off his religion unless he lays off himself. Our religion should be incorporated within ourselves, a part of our being that cannot be laid off. If there can be such a thing as a man laying off his religion, the moment he does so he gets onto ground he knows nothing about, he gives himself over to the powers of darkness. (9 October 1867, JD, 12:148.)

A strong character is an asset in the spirit world. I am under the strongest impression that the most valuable consideration, and that which will be of the most service when we return to the spirit world, will be that of having established a proper and well-defined character as faithful and consistent Latter-day Saints in this state of probation. (6 May 1882, JD, 23:189.)

The Latter-day Saints need repetition. It is like the schoolboy, however, when he commences to learn the alphabet. The letter *A* is pointed out to him by the teacher, and tells him what it is and asks him to please remember it. The next letter, *B,* is pointed out, and the boy is asked to remember that. The teacher then returns to *A.* What letter is that? The boy has forgotten and it has to be repeated by the teacher. Will you please remember it now? The boy says, "O yes, I'll remember it." He feels sure that he can remember it now. But when the teacher returns to the letter once more, the boy has forgotten it again. So they go through the alphabet, having to repeat each letter over and over again. It is the same with the Latter-day Saints. We have to talk to them, and keep talking to them. (7 October 1899, CR, p. 27.)

We must learn by experience. Sailors and mariners become wise, useful, and qualified for their stations only by experience. Storms, tempests, and hurricanes have to occur in order to give them that experience. If all was calm, and storms never arose at sea, where would the mariner get the experience that is necessary for him to have, that when storms do occur and difficulties arise, when the ship sails out upon the ocean, he shall be prepared to manage and guide his vessel safely into port? If there are individuals on board that have never experienced storms, or perhaps have never ventured away from land before, when storms arise, you see that trepidation of spirit that you do not witness in those that have had experience.

So it is with ourselves in the gospel of Jesus Christ: we have to learn by the things that take place around us and act in the stations assigned us by the circumstances that transpire and the experience we gain. (7 October 1857, JD, 5:322.)

The Lord will not prosper the uncharitable. Yet here are men among us who call themselves Latter-day Saints, who do not impart of their substance according to the law of the gospel. I say God is displeased with such covetousness, and He will never prosper the Latter-day Saints who are guilty of such miserly conduct. (19 October 1879, JD, 20:368.)

We should feel gratitude regardless of our circumstances. I have thought sometimes that one of the greatest virtues the Latter-day Saints could possess is gratitude to our Heavenly Father for that which He has bestowed upon us and the path over which He has led us. It may be that walking along in that path has not always been of the most pleasant character; but we have afterwards discovered that those circumstances which have been very unpleasant have often proved of the highest advantage to us. We should always be pleased with the circumstances that surround us and that which the Lord requires at our hands. (6 April 1899, CR, p. 2.)

Our blessings depend on whether we obey or ignore the gospel. When these things were opened up to our view—the principles of the gospel and the glory of the celestial worlds—it was then our privilege to enjoy its blessings to a certain extent, just as though we had been translated into the celestial worlds; it was our privilege to enjoy a certain amount of the blessings that pertain to those laws. And just so far as we have conformed to these laws that pertain to our temporal salvation, just so far as we have obeyed the instructions given to us in regard to our temporal union, just so far we stand in prosperity before God and before the world; just so far as we have been induced to open our hearts to display the principles of philanthropy in the exercise of our religion, just so far do we stand this day approved of the Almighty God; just so far have we secured the implements or the means to defend ourselves against the approaching evils; just so far in all our settlements, cities, towns, or villages, as we have observed these laws that pertain to our temporal obligations, just so far has prosperity attended our exertions, and just so far as the spirit of union prevailed in our midst, and we have advanced ourselves in these principles. And just so far as we have ignored these things, just so far do we stand weak today before God and before the world. (8 April 1880, CR, p. 80.)

This, then, was the gospel order in the days of the Apostles— belief on Jesus Christ, repentance, baptism by immersion for the remission of sins, and the laying on of hands for the reception of the Holy Ghost. When this order was understood and properly attended to, power, gifts, blessings, and glorious privileges followed immediately; and, in every age and period, when these steps are properly attended to, and observed in their proper place and order, the same blessings are sure to follow; but, when neglected, either wholly or in part, there will be either an entire absence of those blessings or a great diminishing of them. (1841, SML, p. 84.)

CHAPTER 4

Knowledge: That Which Matters Most

Knowledge from God is perfect. I dare say that the people that are before me this morning have learned that it was an absolute necessity to have a perfect understanding, and an understanding that could only come directly from the Lord. It would not be satisfactory simply to turn over the leaves of the New Testament and to see that these principles were in accordance with those preached by the Apostles of old, but to have this knowledge come directly to themselves from the Lord. Now, I say this in order that if there are any Latter-day Saints, who have not advanced to this knowledge and cannot see and understand clearly that they have espoused the principles of salvation and exaltation and glory, and that directly from the Lord, it is time they were about receiving this information. (5 October 1900, CR, p. 2.)

We should progress spiritually, intellectually, and physically. We ought to understand that we have espoused a system of religion that is calculated in its nature to increase within us wisdom and knowledge; that we have entered upon a path that is progressive, that will increase our spiritual, intellectual, and physical advantages, and everything pertaining to our own happiness and the well-being of the world at large. (14 January 1872, JD, 14:300.)

The whole idea of Mormonism is improvement—mentally, physically, morally, and spiritually. No half-way education suffices for the Latter-day Saint. He holds with Herbert Spencer that the function of education is to "prepare man for complete living," but he also maintains that "complete living" should be interpreted "life here and hereafter." Joseph Smith declared that the glory of God is intelligence, that a man is saved no faster than he gets knowledge, and that whatever principles of intelligence he attains to in this life, they will rise with him in the resurrection, giving him the advantage over ignorance and evil in the world to come. He taught that man by constantly progressing may eventually develop into a divine being, like unto his Father in Heaven. (2 January 1902, MS, 64:20-21.)

Spiritual knowledge is the best kind. A little spiritual knowledge is a great deal better than mere opinions and notions and ideas, or even very elaborate arguments; a little spiritual knowledge is very important and of the highest consideration. (5 October 1882, JD, 23:293.)

Serve the Lord and receive knowledge. Now, when a person receives intelligence from the Lord, and is willing to communicate that for the benefit of the people, he will receive continual additions to that intelligence; and there is no end to his increase so long as he will hold fast to the faith of the Lord Jesus Christ; and so long as he will hold himself in readiness to operate here, go there, and work for the Lord, travel abroad to the nations of the earth, or to travel among the mountains of Israel, that individual is bound to become strong and mighty in the power of God and in the intelligence of eternity. (9 April 1857, JD, 5:64.)

We should learn every day. In this system of religion that you and I have received there is something grand and glorious, and something new to learn every day, that is of great value. And it is not only our privilege but it is necessary that we receive these things and gather these new ideas. (6 April 1898, CR, p. 13.)

We have sufficient knowledge available. A sufficiency of information has been placed before us in the revelations of former days, in the revelations to us at the present time to guide us in all of our affairs, both spiritual and temporal, to guide us even to the celestial kingdom to receive of the fulness of the Father. (8 April 1880, CR, p. 80.)

Only knowledge brings permanent happiness. There are some who do not learn and who do not improve as fast as they might, because their eyes and their hearts are not upon God. They do not reflect, neither do they have that knowledge which they might have; they miss a good deal which they might receive. We have got to obtain knowledge before we obtain permanent happiness; we have got to be wide awake to the things of God.

Though we may now neglect to improve our time, to brighten up our intellectual faculties, we shall be obliged to improve them sometime. We have got so much ground to walk over; and if we fail to travel today, we shall have so much more to travel tomorrow. (11 October 1857, JD, 5:314.)

Obedience brings knowledge. Let the power that God has put into our hands be used; for herein lies a continued advancement in dominion, in power, and in knowledge. We should be ready at all times to exercise all the power, means, and influence we possess in the service of our God, and resignedly follow out the directions of our President and those that are appointed over us.

Let us be like little children, ready and willing to do as we are commanded by the powers that we should obey. Let us be obedient to the voice of truth, and ever be found in the path of duty; and there let us continue. Let a man do this, and he continues to advance; he will grow in the knowledge of God, and in influence, and in everything that is good. We may well be said to be a people of one mind, for we are the Saints of the living God. The Saints who are brought from the nations of the earth—those who have been gathered together in one, are the ones who hold the birthright to reign on the earth. (11 October 1857, JD, 5:314.)

Knowledge comes by exertion. It is impossible to advance in the principles of truth, to increase in heavenly knowledge, except we exercise our reasoning faculties and exert ourselves in a proper manner. We have an instance recorded in the Doctrine and Covenants of a misunderstanding on the part of Oliver Cowdery, touching this principle. The Lord promised him the gift to translate ancient records. Like many of us today, he had misconceptions in regard to the exercise of the gift. He thought all that was necessary for him to do, inasmuch as this gift had been promised him of God, was to allow his mind to wait in idleness without effort, until it should operate spontaneously. But when those records were placed before him, there was no knowledge communicated, they still remained sealed, as it were, for no power to translate came upon him.

Although the gift to translate had been conferred, he could not prosecute the work, simply because he failed to exert himself before God with the view of developing the gift within him. . . .

So in regard to us, respecting the things which we are undertaking. If we expect to improve, to advance in the work immediately before us, and finally to obtain possession of those gifts and glories, coming up to that condition of exaltation we anticipate, we must take thought and reflect, we must exert ourselves, and that too to the utmost of our ability. (5 April 1877, JD, 18:371-72.)

Man learns by degrees. It is a good thing, brethren, to be a Saint. We are as children; we have to pass through the state of infancy, of childhood, and of youth, before we can arrive at manhood; and we have to learn by degrees. (11 October 1857, JD, 5:314.)

Seek a full knowledge. The time is come when it behooves every man and every woman to know for themselves in relation to the foundation on which they stand. We should all strive to get a little nearer to the Lord. It is necessary for us to advance a little and obtain a full knowledge of those things which we should more fully understand. (18 April 1887, MS, 49:244.)

Knowledge helps us withstand difficulties. God bless this people is my prayer continually, especially in the obtaining of knowledge and intelligence from heaven, so that we may be able to withstand the difficulties, trials, and afflictions which may arise in our path. (5 October 1889, JH, p. 5.)

Suffering brings knowledge. It is profitable to live long upon the earth and to gain the experience and knowledge incident thereto; for the Lord has told us that whatever intelligence we attain to in this life will rise with us in the resurrection, and the more knowledge and intelligence a person gains in this life the greater advantage he will have in the world to come. Some things we have to learn by that which we suffer, and knowledge secured in that way, though the process may be painful, will be of great value to us in the other life. (2 July 1901, JH, p. 5.)

We learn by sharing our knowledge with others. In pursuing any kind of study, a man has to continue to work, and after going through one course, he has to go through again, and keep at work in order to make himself master of them, and he never will master them near so well as by communicating his information while engaged in gaining it. Let him go to work and gather up his friends, and endeavor to give them the same knowledge that he has received, and he then begins to find himself being enlightened upon those things which he never would have known unless by pursuing that course of teaching, and imparting the information he is in possession of unto others. Anyone that has been a schoolteacher will understand me well upon this point. (1 March 1857, JD, 4:241.)

Knowledge cannot be taken from the Saints. When men of integrity, men of honesty, receive a knowledge of any . . . divine principle, when they receive a manifestation of the Almighty concerning the truth of any work or any doctrine, it is a very difficult matter to destroy or force that knowledge from them. You cannot do it by imprisonment, you cannot by any method of torture. So in regard to the people called Latter-day Saints. (6 October 1879, JD, 20:332.)

Ignorance causes displeasure with the commandments. It is because we do not get to understand the requirements of God that we are dissatisfied. God fixes these matters up and arranges them in such a way as will tend to the exaltation of every Latter-day Saint who is disposed to honor them. It is because of our ignorance that we are displeased with the requirements of the Lord. (19 October 1879, JD, 20:367.)

CHAPTER 5

Progressing Toward Perfection

Perfection comes in stages. When the Latter-day Saints received the gospel in the nations afar, and when the voice of the Almighty to them was to leave the lands of their fathers, to leave their kindred as Abraham did, so far as they complied with this requirement, so far they were walking in obedience to this law; and they were as perfect as men could be under the circumstances, and in the sphere in which they were acting; not that they were perfect in knowledge or power, etc., but in their feelings, in their integrity, motives, and determination. And while they were crossing the great deep, providing they did not murmur nor complain, but obeyed the counsels which were given them, and in every way comported themselves in a becoming manner, they were as perfect as God required them to be.

The Lord designs to bring us up into the celestial kingdom. He has made known, through direct revelation, that we are His offspring, begotten in the eternal worlds; that we have come to this earth for the special purpose of preparing ourselves to receive a fulness of our Father's glory when we shall return into His presence. Therefore, we must seek the ability to keep this law, to sanctify our motives, desires, feelings, and affections, that they may be pure and holy, and our will in all things be subservient to the will of God, and have no will of our own except to do the will of our Father. Such a man in his sphere is perfect, and commands the blessing of God in all that he does and wherever he goes. But we are subject to folly, to the weakness of the flesh, and we are more or less ignorant, thereby liable to err. Yes, but that is no reason why we should not feel desirous to comply with this command of God, especially seeing that He has placed within our reach the means of accomplishing this work. This I understand is the meaning of the word perfection, as expressed by our Savior and by the Lord to Abraham. A person may be perfect in regard to some things and not others. A person who obeys the Word of Wisdom faithfully is perfect as far as that law is concerned. When we repented of our sins and were baptized for the remission of them, we were perfect as far as that matter was concerned. Now, we are told by the Apostle John that "we are the sons of God, but it does not appear what we shall be; but we know that when he shall appear, we shall be like him; for we shall see him as he is." (7 April 1879, JD, 20:189.)

When we are overcome we should try again. The Latter-day Saints expect to arrive at this state of perfection; we expect to become as our Father and God, fit and worthy children to dwell in His presence; we expect that when the Son of God shall appear, we shall receive our bodies renewed and glorified, and that "these vile bodies will be changed and become like unto his glorious body." These are our expectations. Now let all present put this question to themselves: Are our expectations well founded? In other words, are we seeking to purify ourselves? How can a Latter-day Saint feel justified in himself unless he is seeking to purify himself even as God is pure—unless he is seeking to keep his conscience void of offense before God and man every day of his life? We doubtless, many of us, walk from day to day, and from week to week, and from month to month, before God, feeling under no condemnation, comporting ourselves properly, and seeking earnestly and in all meekness for the Spirit of God to dictate our daily course; and yet there may be a certain time or times in our life, when we are greatly tried and perhaps overcome; even if this be so, that is no reason why we should not try again, and that, too, with redoubled energy and determination to accomplish our object. (7 April 1879, JD, 20:189-90.)

Peter and Abraham achieved gradual perfection. There was the Apostle Peter, for instance, a man valiant for the truth, and a man who walked before God in a manner that met with His divine approval; he told the Savior on a certain occasion that though all men forsook Him he would not. But the Savior, foreseeing what would happen, told him that on that same night, before the cock crowed, he would deny Him thrice and he did so. He proved himself unequal for the trial; but afterwards he gained power, and his mind was disciplined to that extent that such trials could not possibly affect him. And if we could read in detail the life of Abraham, or the lives of other great and holy men, we would doubtless find that their efforts to be righteous were not always crowned with success. Hence we should not be discouraged if we should be overcome in a weak moment; but, on the contrary, straightway repent of the error or the wrong we may have committed, and as far as possible repair it, and then seek to God for renewed strength to go on and do better.

Abraham could walk perfectly before God day after day when he was leaving his father's house, and he showed evidences of a superior and well-disciplined mind in the course he suggested when his herdsmen quarreled with the herdsmen of his nephew Lot. There came a time in Abraham's life, however, which must have been very trying; in fact anything more severe can scarcely be conceived of; that was when the Lord called upon him to offer as a sacrifice his beloved and only son, even him through whom he expected the fulfillment of the great promise made him by the Lord. But through manifesting a proper disposition he was enabled to surmount the trial, and prove his faith and integrity to God. It can hardly be supposed that Abraham inherited such a state of mind from his idolatrous parents; but it is consistent to believe that under the blessing of God he was enabled to acquire it, after going through a similar warfare with the flesh as we are, and doubtless being overcome at times and then overcoming until he was enabled to stand so severe a test. "Let this same mind be in you," says the Apostle Paul, "which was also in Christ Jesus; who being in the form of God, thought it not robbery to be equal with God." Now every man that has this object before him will purify himself as God is pure, and try to walk perfectly before Him. (7 April 1879, JD, 20:190.)

Seek perfection as fast as possible. We have our little follies and our weaknesses; we should try to overcome them as fast as possible, and we should inculcate this feeling in the hearts of our children, that the fear of God may grow up with them from their very youth, and that they may learn to comport themselves properly before Him under all circumstances. If the husband can live with his wife one day without quarreling or without treating anyone unkindly or without grieving the Spirit of God in any way, that is well so far; he is so far perfect. Then let him try to be the same the next day. But supposing he should fail in this his next day's attempt! That is no reason why he should not succeed in doing so the third day. (7 April 1879, JD, 20:190-91.)

Do not be discouraged. If the Apostle Peter had become discouraged at his manifest failure to maintain the position that he had taken to stand by the Savior under all circumstances, he would have lost all; whereas, by repenting and persevering he lost nothing but gained all, leaving us too to profit by his experience. The Latter-day Saints should cultivate this ambition constantly which was so clearly set forth by the Apostles in former days. We should try to walk each day so that our conscience would be void of offense before everybody. And God has placed in the Church certain means by which we can be assisted, namely, Apostles, and prophets, and evangelists, etc., "for the perfecting of the Saints," etc. And He has also conferred upon us His Holy Spirit, which is an unerring guide, standing, as an angel of God, at our side, telling us what to do, and affording us strength and succor when adverse circumstances arise in our way. We must not allow ourselves to be discouraged whenever we discover our weakness.

We can scarcely find an instance in all the glorious examples set us by the prophets, ancient or modern, wherein they permitted the evil one to discourage them; but on the other hand they constantly sought to overcome, to win the prize, and thus prepare themselves for a fulness of glory. The prophet Elijah succeeded. He so walked before God that he was worthy to be translated. And Enoch was found worthy to walk with God some 300 years, and was at last, with his people, taken up to heaven. (7 April 1879, JD, 20:191.)

Seek to be perfect, as our Father is. We are told that in the latter days "there shall be no more thence an infant of days, nor an old man that hath not filled his days; for the child shall die an hundred years old." And in another scripture we are told that the age of the infant shall be as the age of a tree, and that it shall not die until it shall be old, and then it shall not slumber in the dust but be changed in the twinkling of an eye. But in those days people must live perfectly before the Lord, for we are told in the same passage, that "the sinner," instead of being favored, "being an hundred years old, shall be accursed." When we once get it into our minds that we really have the power within ourselves through the gospel we have received to conquer our passions, our appetites, and in all things submit our will to the will of our Heavenly Father, and, instead of being the means of generating unpleasant feelings in our family circle, and those with whom we are associated, but assisting greatly to create a little heaven upon earth, then the battle may be said to be half won. One of the chief difficulties that many suffer from is, that we are too apt to forget the great object of life, the motive of our Heavenly Father in sending us here to put on mortality, as well as the holy calling with which we have been called; and hence, instead of rising above the little transitory things of time, we too often allow ourselves to come down to the level of the world without availing ourselves of the divine help which God has instituted, which alone can enable us to overcome them. We are no better than the rest of the world if we do not cultivate the feeling to be perfect, even as our Father in heaven is perfect. (7 April 1879, JD, 20:191.)

Ultimate perfection is possible. If I were asked to name the greatest achievement of Mormonism, however, I should have to speak of its spiritual triumphs, manifest in its effects upon the lives, characters, and disposition of its converts; in the wonderful religious awakening and reformation that has taken place in their souls as the result of the acceptance and practice of its principles. The great hope that has been kindled in their hearts; the expulsion of doubt; the assurance that their sins are forgiven and washed away; that through the medium of the Holy Spirit they are actually brought into communion with God; the promise not only of salvation, but of exaltation in the life to come, conditioned upon obedience and faithfulness here; the knowledge imparted of the pre-existence and the hereafter, the perpetuity in heaven of family relationships formed on earth, man's true relationship to God, with all that it implies in the way of progress and ultimate perfection—all these give a peace, a sense of security to the soul, a moral and spiritual elevation that passes understanding and constitutes the greatest boon that religion can bestow. (2 January 1902, MS, 64:23.)

The Lord has established laws to produce perfection. The design of the Lord in regard to ourselves, in regard to His people generally, is to bring them to that state and fulness of knowledge, and to that perfection which their spiritual organizations are susceptible of receiving or arriving at. There are certain laws established from all eternity for the purpose of effecting this object. (18 January 1857, JD, 4:183.)

The Lord will not require the impossible. The Lord never has, nor will He require things of His children which it is impossible for them to perform. (7 April 1879, JD, 20:192.)

Try hourly to be perfect. Try, keep trying daily and hourly in all your avocations, in all your walks of life, in all your associations, to be perfect, even as our Father in Heaven is perfect. (May 1884, BLS, p. 486.)

Perfection requires constant rapport with the Spirit. In order to arrive at the state of perfection that David did when he poured out his soul to the Lord in the prayer that I have referred to ("Search me, O God, and know my heart; try me, and know my thoughts; and see if there be any wicked way in me"), we must be true men and true women; we must have faith largely developed, and we must be worthy of the companionship of the Holy Ghost to aid us in the work of righteousness all the day long, to enable us to sacrifice our own will to the will of the Father, to battle against our fallen nature, and to do right for the love of doing right, keeping our eye single to the honor and glory of God. To do this there must be an inward feeling of the mind that is conscious of the responsibility that we are under, that recognizes the fact that the eye of God is upon us and that our every act and the motives that prompt it must be accounted for; and we must be constantly *en rapport* with the Spirit of the Lord. (6 May 1882, JD, 23:190-91.)

We should set our hearts on things above. Jesus when on earth said to His disciples: "Be ye perfect, even as your Father in heaven is perfect." This is what we should all strive after. There is no necessity for Latter-day Saints to worry over the things of this world. They will all pass away. Our hearts should be set on things above; to strive after that perfection which was in Christ Jesus, who was perfectly obedient in all things unto the Father, and so obtained His great exaltation and became a pattern unto His brethren. Why should we fret and worry over these temporal things when our destiny is so grand and glorious? If we will cleave unto the Lord, keep His commandments, pattern after His perfections and reach out unto the eternal realities of His heavenly kingdom, all will be well with us and we shall triumph and obtain the victory in the end. (8 October 1898, DW, 57:513.)

The Saints should prepare to be called from life. All men and women who are worthy to be called Latter-day Saints should live hour by hour in such a way that if they should be called suddenly from this life into the next they would be prepared. The preparation should be such that we should not fear to be called away suddenly into the spirit life. It is our privilege to so live as to have the spirit of light and intelligence to that extent that we shall feel satisfied that all will be well if we should be called away at any hour. (6 October 1899, CR, p. 2.)

We must conform to the will of God. In order for us to effect the purposes of God, we shall have to do as Jesus did—conform our individual will to the will of God, not only in one thing, but in all things, and to live so that the will of God shall be in us. We have the same priesthood that Jesus had, and we have got to do as He did, to make sacrifice of our own desires and feelings as He did; perhaps not to die martyrs as He did, but we have got to make sacrifices in order to carry out the purposes of God, or we shall not be worthy of this holy priesthood, and be saviors of the world. (4 November 1882, JD, 23:341-42.)

It is our duty to be perfect. It certainly is possible to advance ourselves toward the perfections of the Almighty to a very considerable extent, to say the least. In fact, we are commanded to be perfect, even as our Father in Heaven is perfect. From everything that arises, whether it be of a disagreeable nature or of a pleasant character, we should derive information and secure power to serve ourselves in the path of exaltation and glory over which we are moving. (6 October 1898, CR, p. 2.)

We ought to improve ourselves and move faster toward the point of perfection. It is said that we cannot be perfect. Jesus has commanded us to be perfect even as God, the Father, is perfect. It is our duty to try to be perfect, and it is our duty to improve each day, and look upon our course last week and do things better this week; do things better today than we did them yesterday, and go on and on from one degree of righteousness to another. (6 April 1898, CR, pp. 13-14.)

CHAPTER 6

Obedience and Dedication

The Lord expects obedience. Well, my brethren and sisters, I desire to encourage you in the work of righteousness. I feel to bless you. It is the desire of the First Presidency that you may be blessed. We wish to bear with the people in their weaknesses and frailties. We also desire that you will bear with our weaknesses and infirmities. We want to be forgiving and kind towards the Latter-day Saints. We ask them to be lenient and charitable towards us. The Lord wishes to show leniency towards His children on earth, but He requires of them true repentance when they transgress or fail in any duty. He expects their obedience and that they will endeavor to cast aside all sin, to purify themselves and become indeed His people, His Saints, so that they may be prepared to come into His presence, be made like unto Him in all things and reign with Him in His glory. To accomplish this they must walk in the strait and narrow way, making their lives brighter and better, being filled with faith and charity, which is the pure love of Christ, and attending faithfully to every duty in the gospel. (8 October 1898, DW, 57:514.)

Obey God under all circumstances. This work in which you and I are engaged can only prosper and be forwarded through the blessings of God upon our faithful and honest exertions and our determination to accomplish the labors for which we have come into this existence. When we look back upon the experiences through which we have passed, we easily understand that our prosperity has been dependent upon our honest endeavors to accomplish the work of God, to labor in the interest of the people, and to rid ourselves as far as possible of selfishness. This having been so in the past, we can well believe that our future progress will depend upon our determination to do the will of God under all circumstances, and the aid which He shall give to us. (5 April 1901, CR, p. 1.)

Obedience brings blessing. The Lord has placed before us incentives of the grandest character. In the revelations which God has given, we find what a person can reach who will travel this path of knowledge and be guided by the Spirit of God. I had not been in this Church more than two years when it was clearly shown to me what a man could reach through a continued obedience to the gospel of the Son of God. That knowledge has been as a star continually before me, and has caused me to be particular in trying to do that which was right and acceptable to God. (3 November 1894, DW, 49:609.)

Obedience always precedes blessings. In early ages of the world, also in the days of the Apostles, people came into possession of spiritual powers and various privileges by obtaining an understanding of, and faithfully attending to, certain rules which the Lord established; as, for instance, Abel, obtaining information that offering up sacrifices was an order instituted of God, through which men might receive blessing, he set himself to work, observed the order, and performed the sacrifice, whereby he obtained glorious manifestations of the Most High. Again, when the antediluvians had corrupted themselves, and the time arriving at which destruction was coming upon them, the Lord revealed a course whereby the righteous might escape; accordingly, all who understood and observed that course, were sure to realize the blessing promised. Joshua, before obtaining possession of Jericho, had to observe certain steps appointed of God. The steps having been properly taken, according to commandment, the object immediately fell into his possession. Another instance: the case of Naaman, captain of the Syrian host. It appears that being afflicted with the leprosy and hearing of Elisha the prophet, he made application to him for the removal of that affliction. The prophet, having the Holy Ghost upon him, informed him that by washing in Jordan's waters seven times he might be restored. At first, Naaman thought this too simple and was displeased, and disposed not to conform— not to make use of means so simple. After due consideration, however, humbling himself, he went forth complying with the rules; when, lo! the blessing directly followed. (1841, SML, p. 77.)

We should be devoted, not lukewarm. Knowing our religion to be true, we ought to be the most devoted people on the face of the earth to the cause we have embraced. Knowing as we do, or should know, that the gospel we have received promises all our hearts can wish or desire, if we are faithful, we ought to be very faithful, devoted, energetic, and ambitious in carrying out the designs and wishes of the Lord, as He reveals them from time to time through His servants. We ought not to be lukewarm, or negligent in attending to our duties, but with all our might, strength, and souls we should try to understand the spirit of our calling and nature of the work in which we are engaged. (9 October 1867, JD, 12:146.)

Living the gospel requires determination. We should strive earnestly to establish the principles of heaven within us, rather than trouble ourselves in fostering anxieties like the foolish people of the Tower of Babel, to reach its location before we are properly and lawfully prepared to become its inhabitants. Its advantages and blessings, in a measure, can be obtained in this probationary state by learning to live in conformity with its laws and the practice of its principles. To do this, there must be a feeling and determination to do God's will. (6 May 1882, JD, 23:191.)

We must dedicate our time, talents, and ability. If we as elders fail to keep the covenants we have made, namely, to use our time, talents, and ability for the upbuilding of the kingdom of God upon the earth, how can we reasonably expect to come forth in the morning of the First Resurrection, identified with the great work of redemption? If we in our manner, habits and dealings, imitate the Gentile world, thereby identifying ourselves with the world, do you think, my brethren, that God will bestow upon us the blessings we desire to inherit? I tell you no, He will not! In all our business occupations we must prove ourselves better than any other people, or we forfeit all. We must build ourselves up in the righteousness of heaven and plant in our hearts the righteousness of God. Said the Lord, through the prophet Jeremiah, "I will put my law in their inward parts, and write it in their hearts; and will be their God, and they shall be my people." This is what the Lord is endeavoring to do, and this He will accomplish in us if we conform to His will. (31 January 1877, DN, 25:834.)

Be ready to live or die for truth. When the three Hebrew children, for instance, had been brought to a certain position, cast into the fiery furnace because of their undying faith and integrity, they could not after all perhaps have been placed in more pleasing and agreeable circumstances. A holy being, it is said, appeared and walked with them, side by side in the midst of the flames; and so with Daniel under similar circumstances. Did they wait to see what God would do for them? No; it was "move on" with them. They knew that in the hands of their Master were held the issues of life and death, and that to die in Him is to live, live eternally, to go on, on to perfection until they should become even like unto Him; and having a living, an abiding faith, and a knowledge of the true and living God, they were ready to live and they were ready to die for the truth. (7 April 1882, JD, 23:153.)

Our desire should be to do God's will. Jesus said: "Verily, verily, I say unto you, The Son can do nothing of himself, but what he seeth the Father do: for what things soever he doeth, these also doeth the Son likewise" (John 5:19). He came into this life to do the will of His father, and not His own will. Our desire and determination should be the same. When things come up that require an exertion on our part, we should bring our wills into subjection to the will of the Father, and feel to say, what is the will of our Father, whom we have here in the world to serve? Then every act that we perform will be a success. We may not see its success today or tomorrow, nevertheless it will result in success. (6 October 1899, CR, p. 2.)

Perform your duties in spite of difficulties. Do not falter; continue to do your duty, whatever it may be, whether pleasing or displeasing; be the servants and handmaidens of God to the very utmost. In the past His blessings have been upon us just so far as we have served Him in faithfulness; they will be so in the future. There is no occasion for any man who has the manifestation of the Lord in this line to be discouraged. When our surroundings are not so agreeable as might be wished, think how much worse they might be. Be contented with our conditions. Improve them when opportunity arises, but do not worry about them. (5 April 1901, CR, p. 3.)

We must exert ourselves until our duties become natural. An individual, undertaking to learn to play upon a flute, at first finds a difficulty in making the notes; and in order to play a tune correctly there is a great deal of diligence and patience required. He has to go on, to pause, to turn back and commence afresh. But after a time he is enabled, through a great deal of exertions, to master that tune. When called upon to play that tune afterwards, there is no necessity for remembering where to place the fingers, but he plays it naturally. It was not natural at the first; there had to be a great deal of patience and labour, before it became natural to go through with the tune.

It is just so in regard to matters that pertain to the things of God. We have to exert ourselves and go from grace to grace, to get the law of action so incorporated in our systems, that it may be natural to do those things that are required of us. The son cannot always see the intrinsic benefit of a father's counsel when it is given, but that which he does know is that his father has a right to give that counsel; he also knows that he is in duty bound to act in accordance with that counsel and that knowledge. By acting in that way he will feel well, and he will do his duty. (18 January 1857, JD, 4:186-87.)

Never stand still. I would say, let the motto be to every elder in Israel, and to every person worthy to be called a Saint: "Fear not, and never stand still, but move on." Let the farmer go forward making improvements, plow and sow and reap; and those engaged in proper and useful enterprises continue to do what seems good according to the Spirit of God that may operate upon them, and let every man be faithful and very diligent in keeping the commandments of God, and cultivate the desire to do good to those around him; and if, in reflecting on the past, we find we have not acted strictly in accordance with the dictates of our consciences and duty, let us make ourselves right before God and man, that we may be prepared for every event that may transpire. (7 April 1882, JD, 23:152.)

There is no stopping place in the Lord's program. It may appear through our ignorance in not understanding fully the ways of the Lord and His purposes, that in our onward march in carrying out the program before us, we sometimes come to a stopping place for the time being. But the fact is, there is no such thing in the program—and there cannot be, providing the people continue their labors putting their trust in the promises of God. (7 April 1882, JD, 23:152.)

Devoting ourselves to God brings success. There is a course for every person to pursue in which there will be no failure. It will apply to temporal as well as spiritual matters. The Lord has given us the keyword in these verses that I have read from the Doctrine and Covenants: "If your eye be single to my glory, your whole bodies shall be filled with light, and there shall be no darkness in you; and that body which is filled with light comprehendeth all things. Therefore, sanctify yourselves that your minds become single to God." That is the key by which a person can always be successful. (12 May 1894, DW, 48:637.)

I pray that I may always serve the Lord. This is what I ask my Father in yonder worlds, that my circumstances ever may be such that I can perform His work and labor as an active agent in His hands to accomplish His purposes on the earth. (18 April 1887, MS, 49:243.)

The faithful will receive all that the Father has. I devoted myself to be worthy to receive something that no mortal man can receive except through the spirit and power of the Holy Ghost, and the Lord has shown me things and made me to understand them as clearly as the sun at noonday in regard to what shall be the outcome of those Latter-day Saints that are faithful to their callings. Jesus says: "He that receiveth me receiveth my Father; and he that receiveth my Father receiveth my Father's kingdom; therefore all that my Father hath shall be given unto him" (D&C 84:37-38). (10 April 1898, CR, p. 62.)

The faithful will be crowned as kings and queens. God bless the Latter-day Saints and pour out His Spirit upon you. May you be faithful to your God, faithful to your families, and conduct yourselves with prudence in all things, and labor for the interests of the kingdom of God, and that we may not be among the foolish virgins, but be found worthy to be amongst those who will be crowned as kings and queens and reign throughout eternity. (18 April 1887, MS, 49:246.)

We should be diligent in God's service. Having received the light of the everlasting gospel, and partaken of the good things of the kingdom, and being of the seed of Israel and heirs to great and glorious promises, we should labor with fidelity and diligence to accomplish what God has designed to do through us. We should be men and women of faith and power as well as good works; and when we discover ourselves careless or indifferent in the least, it should be sufficient for us to know it in order to mend our ways and return to the path of duty. (6 May 1882, JD, 23:194.)

We should renew our covenants before God and the holy angels that we will, God being our helper, serve Him more faithfully during the ensuing year than we have in the past, that our public and private life, our actions and the spirit and influence we wield may be in keeping with the motto, "The Kingdom of God or nothing." (8 April 1880, CR, p. 81.)

Our great purpose in life is to do the Father's will. We came into the world for a great purpose, the same as Jesus, our elder brother, to do the will and works of our Father. In this there is peace, joy and happiness, an increase of wisdom, knowledge, and the power of God; outside of this are no promised blessings. Thus let us devote ourselves to righteousness, help each and all to be better and happier; do good to all and evil to none; honor God and obey His priesthood; cultivate and preserve an enlightened conscience and follow the Holy Spirit; faint not, hold fast to what is good, endure to the end, and your cup of joy shall be full even to overflowing, for great shall be your reward for your trials and your sufferings under temptations, your fiery ordeals, your heart yearnings and tears; yea, our God will give you a crown of unfading glory, and make you kings and queens in the midst of your posterity, to rule in righteousness through the countless ages of eternities. (May 1884, BLS, p. 487.)

CHAPTER 7

Testimony: A Sure Foundation

Revelation is our sure foundation. We have established our faith upon a sure foundation, and there is no power beneath the celestial worlds that can take it from us. Everyone has the right to secure, and I hope has secured, this principle of revelation upon which we are founded, each for himself or herself. (18 May 1899, MS, 61:530.)

A testimony comes by revelation. To one was given faith, to another knowledge—not that which is gained by reading books merely, but knowledge from the Almighty. A self-inspiring principle was upon them which was tangible, giving them a knowledge of the cause they had espoused. They knew by revelation from God that the cause they had obeyed was true: it was revealed to them in a manner they could not dispute, and they knew for themselves. They were then established, as we heard this morning, upon the rock of revelation. (14 January 1872, JD, 14:303-4.)

The foundation upon which The Church of Jesus Christ of Latter-day Saints is built is the rock of revelation—upon the rock that Jesus said He would build His church, and the gates of hell should not prevail against it. We have not received this knowledge through flesh and blood, we have not received this testimony from man, we have not received it through the reading of the Bible, New Testament, or Book of Mormon, but we have received it through the operations of the Holy Ghost, that teaches of the things of God, things past, present and to come, and that takes of the things of God, making them clearly manifest unto us. You cannot take this knowledge from us by imprisonment or any kind of persecution. We will stand by it unto death. (6 October 1879, JD, 20:332.)

No one can know Jesus is the Christ but by revelation. In the days of Noah the people of that generation had the privilege of knowing whether Noah spoke from the Lord and whether the message that he claimed to have from the Lord was genuine or not. They could have had a revelation for themselves, because he preached the gospel as you and I now preach it in the world, and they could have known that their salvation depended upon their receiving and obeying this message which Noah delivered unto them. In the days of Jesus it was the same. But no person can know that Jesus is the Son of God, except by revelation. (6 April 1900, CR, p. 3.)

The rock of revelation brings peace and security. "Blessed art thou, Simon Barjona: for flesh and blood hath not revealed it unto thee, but my Father which is in heaven. . . . And upon this rock I will build my church; and the gates of hell shall not prevail against it." [Matthew 16:17-18.] Peter had obtained a revelation which Jesus called a Rock, which every man might receive individually for himself to build upon, with perfect assurance and safety—on which he could anchor his hopes and prospects of salvation. Peter, on the day of Pentecost, promised the Holy Ghost to those who would repent and receive baptism. That principle imparts the knowledge or the rock of revelation upon which the Savior declared His people should be established; and we constitute the only religious community which dares assume this scriptural position; and our realization of the Savior's promise, that "hell shall not prevail against" a people thus established, affords us peace, tranquility, unshaken confidence, and a cheering and happy assurance of security in the midst of all kinds of threatened ruin and overthrow. (6 March 1886, JD, 26:376.)

All may have a testimony. Our elders simply affirm having received a divine knowledge of the fact that this gospel was a heaven-born institution, and through its virtue and divine force every honest-hearted man might obtain this same knowledge. I had been a member of this Church but a few days when I obtained—through a divine manifestation—a clear, explicit, and tangible knowledge of the truth of this work. Thousands and tens of thousands of Latter-day Saints, men and women, in private life, could testify to the same experience; and though I may know many things in regard to this doctrine which in their limited experience they may not understand, yet in this one fact they are equal with me in knowledge, equal with the messengers who administered to them this gospel. (23 January 1870, JD, 13:290.)

A testimony prevents deception by men. There is a great difference between the operations of the Latter-day Saints and those of the Christian world. With us there is no deception; nor indeed is there any chance for any. People gather here in thousands on the principle that the Lord God has revealed, and they have an opportunity of knowing, that the Almighty has spoken from the heavens. They are not left to the mere statement of any one. (9 October 1869, JD, 13:258.)

Everyone's faith will be tested. Those persons who received this work without religious motives, and without an honest conviction of its divine requirements, but solely for the "loaves and fishes," cannot possibly abide the test to which everyone's faith, sooner or later, must be brought; but will have his dishonesty and hypocrisy exposed, and will sooner or later apostatize. (6 March 1886, JD, 26:374-75.)

Revealed knowledge withstands all tests. Now you take a man, no matter from what country: if he be a man of integrity, when he receives a knowledge of the truth, he will stand to that knowledge? You cannot persecute it out of him by imprisoning him, or taking away his property, or by destroying every source of his happiness. Do what you can to annoy and oppress him, he will stand firm in his adherence to the principles which he knows are true. (14 January 1872, JD, 14:305.)

The Saints need to receive spiritual and physical manifestations. Now, when we received these principles it was clear to us, I presume, that we actually received assurances, the most perfect assurances, that what was said to us was actually of the Lord, that the parties that brought us these principles were actually inspired from the Most High. The nature and character of the work that each one would necessarily have to perform, the circumstances that would surround us and the trials and temptations to which we had to be exposed, would require a perfect understanding, not through the teachings of these individuals that proclaimed to us these principles, but actual manifestations and assurances that should come from the Lord, either by extraordinary faith or by a perfect reception, physical and spiritual, of the Holy Spirit, a baptism of the Holy Ghost, as was promised in former days to those that should receive the gospel. (5 October 1900, CR, p. 2.)

We should seek to know positively. There is this privilege that every Latter-day Saint should seek to enjoy, to know positively that his work is accepted of God. I am afraid Latter-day Saints are not much better and perhaps they are worse than other people if they do not have this knowledge and seek to do right. (6 April 1898, CR, p. 13.)

No man should be satisfied until he has secured a perfect assurance that this is the path of exaltation and glory; that Joseph Smith was a prophet of God. (1 June 1895, DW, 50:738.)

Latter-day Saints need testimonies in order to advance. We know from our experience that the foundation upon which we have placed our faith is grand and glorious. I know this for myself. I had been in this church but a short time when I succeeded in securing the most perfect knowledge that there was a God, that there was a Son, Jesus Christ, and that Joseph Smith was acknowledged of God as His prophet. It was a knowledge that no man could communicate. It came through a revelation from the Almighty. That is a very good starting point for a Latter-day Saint, and it is something that every person, who has any ambition at all to advance in this path, will need at some time or other. He will come into circumstances of such a nature that he will need strength, and that strength will come from a knowledge of the fact that the path in which he is traveling will lead him to the possession of his highest and best desires. (3 November 1894, DW, 49:609.)

CHAPTER 8

Joseph Smith, the Prophet

I know that Joseph Smith was a prophet of God. A word or two about Joseph Smith. Perhaps there are very few men now living who were so well acquainted with Joseph Smith the Prophet as I was. I was with him oftentimes. I visited with him in his family, sat at his table, associated with him under various circumstances, and had private interviews with him for counsel. I know that Joseph Smith was a prophet of God; I know that he was an honorable man, a moral man, and that he had the respect of those who were acquainted with him. The Lord has shown me most clearly and completely that he was a prophet of God, and that he held the holy priesthood. (7 October 1900, CR, p. 61.)

The mission of Joseph Smith was to preach the gospel. Joseph Smith received a revelation and commandment from the Lord to go forth and preach the gospel of salvation to the nations of the earth, with power and authority to baptize those who would repent of their sins and be immersed in water for the remission of them; he was also commanded to preach the gathering to them, that a people might be drawn together who would be willing to harken to the voice of the Lord and keep His laws, that a righteous seed might thereby be preserved when the great day of His wrath should come. (9 October 1869, JD, 13:254.)

Christ revealed Himself to Joseph Smith. We testify to the whole world that we know, by divine revelation, even through the manifestations of the Holy Ghost, that Jesus is the Christ, the Son of the living God, and that He revealed Himself to Joseph Smith as personally as He did to His Apostles, anciently, after He arose from the tomb, and that He made known unto him those heavenly truths by which alone mankind can be saved. (6 October 1876, JD, 18:298.)

Joseph was chosen by God. Joseph Smith, whom God chose to establish this work, was poor and uneducated, and belonged to no popular denomination of Christians. He was a mere boy, honest, full of integrity, unacquainted with the trickery, cunning and sophistry employed by the politicians and the religious hypocrite to accomplish their ends. Like Moses he felt incompetent and unqualified for the task, to stand forth as a religious reformer, in a position the most unpopular, to battle against opinions and creeds which have stood for ages, having had the sanction of men, the most profound in theological obedience; but God had called him to deliver the poor and honest-hearted of all nations from their spiritual and temporal thraldom. (23 January 1870, JD, 13:287.)

Joseph was devoted to the interest of mankind. Joseph Smith, the Prophet, with whom I was intimately acquainted for years, as well as I was with my brother, I know him to have been a man of integrity, a man devoted to the interests of humanity and to the requirements of God all the days in which he was permitted to live. There never was a man that possessed a higher degree of integrity and more devotedness to the interest of mankind than the Prophet Joseph Smith. I can say this from a personal acquaintance with him. (10 April 1898, CR, p. 64.)

Joseph Smith was an extraordinary man. I had an intimate acquaintance with Joseph Smith, the Prophet, for a number of years. The position he occupied before the world and the declarations which he made were of an extraordinary character. It was a position which no individual before or since has attempted to assume. I know Joseph Smith to have been an honest man, a man of truth, honor, and fidelity, willing to sacrifice everything he possessed, even life itself, as a testimony to the heavens and the world that he had borne the truth to the human family. (5 October 1889, JH, p. 5.)

Joseph said his work was finished. A few months previous to this murder, Joseph, in giving instructions to the Twelve in relation to the building up of Zion, preparatory to the coming of the Son of God, informed them that his work was finished on the earth, and from that time the responsibility of carrying the gospel to every nation devolved upon them; and, as he bid farewell to some friends, on leaving for Carthage, he said: "I am going like a lamb to the slaughter; but I am calm as a summer's morning; I have a conscience void of offence towards God, and towards all men; I shall die innocent, and it shall yet be said of me—he was murdered in cold blood." An intimate acquaintance with those men from the early rise of the Church to their martyrdom, justifies the writer in bearing this testimony that he knows they were virtuous, honorable and righteous men—men whom God loved, and whom all good men would have respected, loved and honored had they known their true character. (1851, BLS, pp. 157-58.)

Joseph Smith was empowered to usher in the fulness of times. Joseph Smith declared that an angel from heaven revealed to him the golden plates of the Book of Mormon, containing the gospel, and that other heavenly messengers ordained him to the Aaronic and Melchizedek Priesthoods, thus empowering him to ordain others, to preach faith and repentance, to baptize by immersion in water for the remission of sins, and to lay on hands for the gift of the Holy Ghost; in short, to do all things necessary to be done to usher in the dispensation of the fulness of times. Included in this declaration was the promise that all who obeyed the gospel should experience the same miraculous gifts and powers that were enjoyed by the disciples anciently. (2 January 1902, MS, 64:2-3.)

CHAPTER 9

Obtaining Happiness

The restored gospel brings happiness. After considering the past, and seeing the improvements we have made, as a people and as individuals, it is a matter of importance to us to consider ourselves, to see whether we are making such progress as is required of us—to learn if we are keeping pace with the times and the improvements that are being made by the leading men of the Church—to find out whether we, as individuals, are improving in the principles of the gospel, whether we are improving in the practice of righteous and holy principles, and whether we are gaining knowledge, wisdom, virtue, and getting a more full understanding of how to make ourselves happy, and thus prepare ourselves for that situation that we expect to occupy in the future.

We are in the world, but we are ignorant. We do not know what will make us happy, or whether we shall receive what we anticipate. We know little or nothing about these things. We seek happiness and that which will make us comfortable, but we do not really understand what will make us happy for time and happy for eternity.

The priesthood has been restored. It has been bestowed upon man, that through that medium all who would like to be good and happy might have the privilege. The gospel tells us how to be great, good, and happy. The Spirit of the gospel of Christ teaches all things that are necessary for our present and future welfare.

We have these objects in view today, and we should continually keep them before us. Look back for twenty-five years, or look back ten years only, and a great many have been in the Church that length of time, and see what we have accomplished. We see farther and comprehend things better; hence we are better prepared for the things that are coming on the earth than we were ten, fifteen, twenty, or twenty-five years ago to know how to be useful—to know how to do things as they should be done.

A man may be a very good man, and yet not have wisdom to do things right; but we have got the Spirit that will enable us to know how to put them in the best channel, so that they will be best calculated to roll on the kingdom of God, to make us happy, and prepare us for the scenes that lie before us. Is not the gospel a good thing? Is it not worthy of a man losing his substance and even his life to gain the blessings that are promised to the faithful in Israel? The man who has the priesthood, who is filled with the Holy Ghost, is to be guided and dictated by it in the way of happiness and life. It is very necessary for us to have these things laid before us frequently, that we may be put in remembrance of our duties.

The organized spirit which God gave us is the one which conceives through the revelations that are given from on high. The nature and the character of those teachings that come from the priesthood are such that we comprehend them; the Spirit manifests them unto us as they are. By it we learn our duties to God and man. We are taught by it to shun the evil and cleave unto that which is good. We understand this, if we are in the path of duty. It is not miracles that produce within us that living faith of which President Young so frequently speaks; but we learn the nature and character of our religion. We learn that which is calculated to enable us to shun all evil power and to make us happy.

When a man receives knowledge, he is prompted to impart it to others; when a man becomes happy, the Spirit that surrounds him teaches him to strive to make others happy. It is not so in the gentile world. If a man attains to any important position, he does not strive to elevate others to participate in the same blessings. In this respect there is a great difference between the Latter-day Saints and the world of mankind. The object of the priesthood is to make all men happy, to diffuse information, to make all partakers of the same blessings in their turn. Is there any chance of a man's becoming happy without a knowledge of the gospel of Christ? A man may make the thunders roll, the lightnings flash; but what has that to do with making a man happy? Nothing. Though in the world they try to make themselves happy, still they are not successful in what they strive to accomplish. They cannot be happy except upon one principle, and that is by embracing the fulness of the gospel, which teaches us not to wait till we get into eternity before we begin to make ourselves happy; but it teaches us to strive here to make ourselves and those around us rejoice in the blessings of the Almighty.

This, then, should be our aim and object: to learn to make ourselves useful—to be saviours to our fellowmen, to learn how to save them, to communicate to them a knowledge of the principles that are necessary to raise them to the same degree of intelligence that we have ourselves.

Men may be very good, and yet they may not be very wise, nor so useful as they might be; but the gospel is given to make us wise, and to enable us to get those things in our minds that are calculated to make us happy. (7 April 1861, JD, 9:20-22.)

The Spirit enables us to fulfill our righteous desires. The Lord has established certain constitutional desires and feelings in our bosoms; and it is so with all mankind—with the whole human family. There are implanted and interwoven in their constitutions certain desires and capacities for enjoyment—desires for certain things that are in their nature calculated to promote our peace and well-being, that answer their feeling and promote their happiness. But how to obtain the gratification of those capacities and desires, the world do not know nor understand. But the Lord has seen fit to put us in the channel and in the way of understanding those things by being faithful and walking in the light of the Holy Spirit, and receiving truth, and eventually coming in possession of everything that our hearts desire in righteousness, to promote our peace and happiness and the highest things that pertain to glory and exaltation in the eternal worlds. (11 October 1857, JD, 5:312.)

There is joy in doing good. We have been sent into the world to do good to others; and in doing good to others we do good to ourselves. We should always keep this in view, the husband in reference to his wife, the wife in reference to her husband, the children in reference to their parents, and the parents in reference to their children. There is always opportunity to do good to one another. When you find yourselves a little gloomy, look around you and find somebody that is in a worse plight than yourself; go to him and find out what the trouble is, then try to remove it with the wisdom which the Lord bestows upon you; and the first thing you know, your gloom is gone, you feel light, the Spirit of the Lord is upon you, and everything seems illuminated. (6 April 1899, CR, pp. 2-3.)

Serve faithfully and be cheerful. Brethren and sisters, the thing you should have in your mind, and which you should make a motto in your life, is this: Serve God faithfully, and be cheerful. I dislike very much, and I believe people generally do, to see a person with a woe begone countenance, and to see him mourning as though his circumstances were of the most unpleasant character. There is no pleasure in association with such persons. In the family it is always a good thing for the parent to be cheerful in the presence of his wife and children. And out of that cheerfulness may arise many good gifts. The Lord has not given us the gospel that we may go around mourning all the days of our lives. He has not introduced this religion for this purpose at all. We came into the world for certain purposes, and those purposes are not of a nature that require much mourning or complaint. Where a person is always complaining and feeling to find fault, the Spirit of the Lord is not very abundant in his heart. If a person wants to enjoy the Spirit of the Lord, let him, when something of a very

disagreeable nature comes along, think how worse the circumstance might be, or think of something worse that he has experienced in the past. Always cultivate a spirit of gratitude. It is
actually the duty of every Latter-day Saint to cultivate a spirit of
gratitude. (3 April 1897, DW, 54:481.)

We should enjoy our religion. No religion has in it such prospects as has the religion of the Latter-day Saints. Nothing was
ever introduced to man equal to it in its grand and glorious advantages. We ought to enjoy our religion to such an extent as to
be happy most all the time. We should never allow ourselves to
get into a position where we cannot secure some happiness. The
prospects that have been opened up to us are grand. In the next
life we will have our bodies glorified and free from sickness and
death. Nothing is so beautiful as a person in a resurrected and
glorified condition. There is nothing more lovely than to be in
this condition and have our wives and children and friends with
us. So long as we are faithful, nothing can prevent us from
getting all the enjoyment that can be secured through prospects
of this kind. Whether we are in prison, or whether we are in
poverty, these prospects are always before us, if we live our
religion. Now, brethren and sisters, be faithful, keep the commandments of God. (7 October 1900, CR, p. 63.)

The light of the Spirit brings happiness. All this trouble and
vexation of mind is but a matter of the present; and if we keep the
light of the Spirit within us, we can so walk in the gospel that we
can measurably enjoy happiness in this world; and while we are
traveling onward, striving for peace and happiness that lie in our
path, in the distance, we shall have a peace of mind that none can
enjoy but those who are filled with the Holy Spirit. (11 October
1857, JD, 5:313.)

Knowledge is necessary for happiness. There are some who do
not learn and who do not improve as fast as they might, because
their eyes and their hearts are not upon God. They do not reflect,

neither do they have that knowledge which they might have; they miss a good deal which they might receive. We have got to obtain knowledge before we obtain permanent happiness; we have got to be wide awake to the things of God. (11 October 1857, JD, 5:314.)

Charity brings happiness. Men and women of wealth, use your riches to give employment to the laborer! Take the idle from the crowded centers of population and place them on the untilled areas that await the hand of industry. Unlock your vaults, unloose your purses, and embark in enterprises that will give work to the unemployed, and relieve the wretchedness that leads to the vice and crime which curse your great cities, and that poison the moral atmosphere around you. Make others happy, and you will be happy yourselves. (1 January 1901, MFP, 3:334.)

Perfect happiness is available to the Saints. There is nothing the Latter-day Saints can imagine that would afford them happiness that God has not unfolded to us. He has prepared everything for the Latter-day Saints that they could possibly wish or imagine in order to effect their complete happiness throughout the vast eternities. (3 April 1897, DW, 54:481.)

There could not be placed before men more glorious prospects than are placed before the Saints. No mortal man could wish anything greater or that will ultimately prove more satisfactory. Everything that pertains to perfect peace, happiness, glory, and exaltation is before the Latter-day Saints. We should enjoy the spirit of this, and keep it actively before us. We should not let our prospects be darkened in the least by doing that which is not acceptable before the Lord. (6 October 1898, CR, p. 3.)

CHAPTER 10

Sharing the Gospel

Our salvation depends on our sharing the gospel. I had never intended to be a preacher, and it was nothing but a perfect knowledge that it was my duty to do so, that I was willing to go forth upon this business—a knowledge that my salvation depended upon my going forth and proclaiming these glad tidings to the world, and I went, and could testify to every man and woman in any nation or community wherever I traveled, that I was authorized to preach the gospel and administer in its ordinances, which pertain to a knowledge of eternal life, a knowledge of time and eternity, and thus establish the divine authenticity of my mission. (18 April 1887, MS, 49:242-43.)

Seeking the salvation of men brings joy and eternal glory. I close by saying to you and the faithful men laboring under your direction, that inasmuch as they shall continually seek unto the Lord in humility, having an eye single to His honor and glory, and desiring in their hearts the salvation of the souls of men, and doing all they can to bring about their salvation, they shall have joy beyond expression in their labors in the flesh, and shall at last be made partakers with the Father and the Son of things too great and glorious for mortality to conceive or contemplate. (12 September 1901, MS, 58:596.)

We should be saviors to our fellowmen. This, then, should be our aim and object: to learn to make ourselves useful, to be saviors to our fellowmen, to learn how to save them, to communicate to them a knowledge of the principles that are necessary to raise them to the same degree of intelligence that we have ourselves. (7 April 1861, JD, 9:22.)

We grow by sharing the gospel. Let a man remember that there are others that are in darkness and that have not advanced so far in knowledge, wisdom, and intelligence, and let him impart that knowledge, intelligence, and power unto his friends and brethren, inasmuch as he is farther advanced than they are, and by so doing he will soon discover that his mind will expand, and that light and knowledge which he had gained would increase and multiply more rapidly.

I have heard Brother [Heber C.] Kimball state that when he was very much downhearted, he would find somebody worse than himself, and endeavor to comfort him up, and by so doing he would comfort himself, and increase in spirit and in life. (1 March 1857, JD, 4:241.)

It is our obligation to spread the gospel. No sooner had the Saints become fairly settled in these valleys than the servants of the Lord turned their attention again to the great missionary work which rested upon the Church.

We were in the midst of poverty and struggling to make the land habitable, but we could not neglect the obligation we were under to spread the gospel abroad; for the Lord had given forth the command that it should be preached in all the world. It is one of the evidences of the divinity of this work that in the midst of all their driving and persecutions the Latter-day Saints have faithfully sought to carry out this command of the Lord. (16 August 1901, JH, p. 5.)

Serving a mission brings honor and glory. In this life we send our missionaries into the world. We select our young men and give them missions to travel among the nations. It is not one of the most pleasant things that might be imagined for a young man to start out, not having had any experience, to go to a land and among a people that he knows nothing at all about, and in many instances does not even understand their language. He realizes that he will have trials, troubles, and difficulties to cope with, and many things of an unpleasant character. In one sense of the word, he parts with his friends unpleasantly; but it is an important duty that he feels now called upon to perform, and there will arise from the performance of these duties honor, and eventually glory and exaltation. (1 June 1895, DW, 50:737-38.)

The Spirit influences elders to serve. It is a strange thing that among the thousands of letters which I have received from those who have been called to go upon missions—mostly young men— I do not think of but one case where a refusal was given. Why is this? It is because the spirit of love and of immortality, the Spirit of the Almighty, is upon these young elders, and they have received manifestations which inspire them to do that which otherwise no inducement could prompt them to do. (5 April 1901, CR, p. 3.)

The missionaries' business is to make people happy. We are laboring, striving, and struggling for the deliverance of the honest in heart throughout the world; we are laboring for the establishment and continuance of holy principles.

There are men on this stand whose testimony you have heard; and those very men would suffer themselves to be cut in pieces, inch by inch, before they would suffer those principles to be trampled upon. It is their business to make people happy—to put them in possession of eternal life, so that sorrowing and crying may cease from the earth. (7 October 1857, JD, 5:324.)

Missionaries should pray for power to save souls. The question will arise, what am I here for? To sow the seeds of life in the hearts of those who are in this audience; and the prayer should arise in your heart, "O Lord, may it be so; may I have power through thy Spirit to touch the hearts of these thy people." That very short prayer is all that an elder needs to make. It is all you need to make. "May I say something to save these souls." This is what the First Presidency and all your brethren want you to do. (December 1899, IE, 3:129.)

Honest hearts appreciate divine truth. This system of religion, in its nature, in the character of its origin, the manner of its operations, and in the purposes for which it was designed, coupled with the fact that people of honest hearts can and will appreciate divine truth, is such that it cannot be destroyed. A man who is honest, full of integrity and love for the interest and happiness of mankind, having explored this long untrodden path, and made this glorious discovery, will not and cannot keep silent, but despite of threats and opposition, however fierce and terrific, will boldly declare the glorious fact, spreading and multiplying this divine intelligence, and if so required, seal this testimony with his own life's blood. (6 March 1886, JD, 26:376.)

Find the way to the hearts of men. The humility you display and the Spirit of the Lord resting upon you, will show your fitness for the position you are called to occupy. Try to understand human nature and act accordingly, in order to make everyone happy and everything agreeable.

I remember an incident related by Brother George A. Smith: He was on a mission, traveling without purse or scrip. He had been turned away from several houses and badly treated. He had always told those to whom he applied for entertainment that he was a "Mormon," and after he had traveled some distance and the day was drawing to a close, he began to fear that he would obtain neither food nor shelter and perhaps be unable to accomplish his mission. In order to avoid this, he concluded to adopt another plan. Journeying a little farther, he came to a house and found the owner putting up a loom. Brother Smith went right to work and assisted him. After they had finished their task, he

began to talk to the man about his stock and his farm, and so
forth. During the conversation, it began to rain, and Brother
Smith, who all this time had not mentioned that he was a "Mormon," started to go, but the man insisted upon his staying to
dinner, and would not permit him to leave his house that night.

There is a way to reach every human heart, and it is your
business to find the way to the hearts of those to whom you are
called on this mission. (December 1899, IE, 3:127-28.)

*The missionaries' love for the people will revolutionize the
world.* The Apostle John remarked in his day, "We know that
we have passed from death unto life, because we love the brethren." This love begotten in the hearts of the missionary elders of
our Church for the peoples of the earth, comparative strangers to
them, and in the hearts of the people for the elders who bear to
them the gospel message, is in itself testimony sufficient to convince the honest heart that its source is divine, and that God is
with us. This sacred and holy feeling, awakened within us by the
Holy Ghost, has already distinguished us as a community from
the rest of the human family; and this is the feeling that will yet
revolutionize the whole world, and convince unbelieving man
that God is not only the Father of us all, but that we are His
friends and servants. I have joy even now in contemplating the
days of my missionary labors. The feelings produced by these
peculiar experiences have become part and parcel of my very
being; and from the nature of things they must necessarily not
only continue to remain so, but to expand and reach out until
they shall find satisfaction in nothing short of the redemption
and salvation of our Father's house. (12 September 1901, MS,
58:595.)

We should do good to those who do not receive the gospel.
Well, we expect to do good; it is our duty, as the servants and
ministers of God upon the earth, to do good to His offspring.
This is our mission, and it is as much our duty to do good to
those who do not receive the gospel, as it is to do good to our-

selves; and God will give us the opportunity, just according to our desires, despite the efforts of evil-minded men. Our business is to save, not to destroy, and as we improve and advance, and develop the attributes of deity within us, God will remove from our path the impediments and obstacles to our progress that are found therein; and the bitter branches, as they increase or manifest themselves, will be removed one after another, until the people of God have all the opportunity they desire to do good to the world. (14 January 1872, JD, 14:309.)

The Lord does not require the impossible. The Lord never has, nor will He require things of His children which it is impossible for them to perform. The elders of Israel who expect to go forth to preach the gospel of salvation in the midst of a crooked and perverse generation, among a people who are full of evil and corruption, should cultivate this spirit especially. (7 April 1879, JD, 20:192.)

The Lord desires to save all men. When the Lord calls an individual or a class of individuals out from the world, it is not always with an object to benefit that particular individual or individuals. The Lord has not in view merely the salvation of a few people called Latter-day Saints, who have been or who may be gathered into these valleys, but the salvation of all men, the living and the dead. (4 November 1882, JD, 23:338.)

The missionaries promise knowledge from God. What is their prediction that is of such high importance to all people? Why, this: Having stated before the congregations of the world that they are authorized to preach the gospel of life and salvation, that they are authorized to promise the gift of the Holy Ghost, that shall lead into all truth and show things to come, and shall testify in reference to their authority, then to make this prediction—that such as will obey the simple principles of the gospel shall receive a perfect knowledge, a knowledge not by the reading of books, the scriptures or any past revelations that may have been given, but they shall receive a knowledge of this from God Himself. (5 October 1897, CR, p. 30.)

Missionary work brings friendships. If you want to secure the friendship and affections of our friends, go to work and comfort them with that light which you have received, remembering those blessings came down from God, and that by doing this you are only doing what every man should do.

Those of you who have got the priesthood, go and make friends among the individuals by whom you are surrounded; or select one and try to start his feelings, his faith, his circumstances, and his mind, and try to enlighten them, and if they are sinners, endeavor to save them from their sins, and bring them from their bondage in which they are placed, to participate in the light and liberty which you participate in, for in this way you can do good through the information which the Lord has imparted to you. In this way you will discover that their minds will be drawn out towards you, and their affections will be gained and centered upon you. (1 March 1857, JD, 4:241.)

Missionaries are ambassadors of heaven. The elders laboring in the vineyard should never lose sight of the fact that they are ambassadors of heaven, bearers of good and glad tidings to peoples who know not the Lord, whose knowledge of Him cannot possibly extend beyond the story told of Him in holy writ. This kind of knowledge is not sufficient either to save or condemn, it being merely hearsay or knowledge born of tradition. (12 September 1901, MS, 58:595.)

Missionary work is God's work. We send our elders to preach the gospel. Who sends them? President Woodruff? In one sense, no. The God of Israel sends them. It is His work. There is no mortal man that is so much interested in the success of an elder when he is preaching the gospel as the Lord that sent him to preach to the people who are the Lord's children. He begot them in yonder world, and they came here because the Lord wanted them to come. (12 May 1894, DW, 48:637.)

Elders should avoid the temptations of the world. I do hope and pray that no elder laboring under your presidency will so far forget himself as to fall a prey to the allurements of the world. There is but one safe way to steer clear of them, and that is to shun evil, yea, even the very appearance of evil. Temptation in some form or other will be presented to them. This is the business of the enemy of our salvation; but it is the business of the elders of Israel to rise above temptation, and in order to do this successfully they must keep themselves unspotted from the world. And I desire to say to them through you, that inasmuch as they cultivate and cherish the spirit of their mission, and realize the importance of their high calling in Christ Jesus, and live in the spirit of the same, they will be able to stand as guides and saviors to the people, reflecting to them the light of heaven, and be unlike other men; but if they trespass on the ground of the enemy and partake of the spirit of the world, they will be shorn of their strength and become like other men, fit only to return home to sup the sorrow of the fallen, and to cause the hearts of their loved ones to mourn because of their condition. (12 September 1901, MS, 58:596.)

Missionaries should not be discouraged. When the Prophet Joseph Smith sent out the first elders to a foreign land, he foresaw the reception that would be accorded them, and he told them that while a comparative few would receive them as God's servants, the masses would reject them, and pay heedless regard to their message. This has been the lot of God's servants from the beginning of time, and we must be content with the results of faithful labors, even if but few through us are brought to a knowledge of the truth. The elders should not be discouraged. They should constantly bear in mind that none cometh to the Son except the Father draweth them; and that therefore, if people cannot receive the Spirit of the Father, they cannot receive the doctrines of His Son, and as a consequence cannot be made partakers with us of the heavenly word. (12 September 1901, MS, 58:596.)

Our influence affects people. You exert a certain degree of influence, and be it ever so small, it affects some person or persons, and for the results of the influence you exert you are held more or less accountable. You, therefore, whether you acknowledge it or not, have assumed an importance before God and man that cannot be overlooked. (6 October 1876, JD, 18:299.)

"I returned and was well entertained." I was once traveling in a strange country on a mission, and had been refused entertainment many times, and my chances for sleeping in a haystack were very good. Presently I came to a hotel. We usually avoided such places, but my affairs were desperate, and I approached the proprietor and told him that I was without means, preaching the gospel, and asked him to give me entertainment. He replied that he was running his hotel to make money, and that I was very welcome to a room in his house and meals at his table upon payment of the regular prices for such commodities. I started to go away, but, upon a little reflection, returned to the man, and again told him that I was a humble elder of the Church of Christ, preaching the gospel, warning the people and calling upon them to repent and turn unto the Lord. I quoted to him the words of the Savior, recorded in Matthew 25:31-46, where He tells of the coming of the Son of Man in His glory, when He shall divide the sheep from the goats and shall bless those on His right hand because they ministered unto Him, but shall cast out those on His left hand, because they ministered not unto Him; and when those on His left hand shall ask when they saw the Son of Man in want and ministered not unto Him, He shall say unto them, "Inasmuch as ye did it not to one of the least of these, ye did it not to me." After having quoted these things, and borne testimony that I was a humble disciple of Jesus Christ, I started to leave him, but he called after me, saying, "Where are you going? Come in here and eat, and stay as long as you desire." I returned and was well

entertained, and no word was ever said to me about paying for the same. (December 1899, IE, 3:128.)

The restored gospel cannot be destroyed. Should the prominent men of this Church, together with tens of thousands of its elders, be swept away by our enemies, the gospel would still survive, and with unabated force and vigor, still continue its irrepressible operations. So long as one solitary elder, however unlearned, obscure or possessing an honest heart, remain alive upon the earth, these holy and sacred truths will be avowed and vindicated, order and proper authority continue their peaceful and happy reign, and elders with hearts overflowing with love and heaven-born zeal, go forth to the nations, churches spring up in every land and clime, Saints increase and multiply and gather together, the kingdom of God continue to be established, and the suggestive and inspired sayings of the prophet Daniel be literally and emphatically accomplished. (23 January 1870, JD, 13:291-92.)

The voice of warning must be sounded. To my brethren in the priesthood I beg to offer a few words of counsel, instruction, and exhortation. Upon you rest high and sacred responsibilities, which relate not only to the salvation of this generation, but of many past generations, and many to come. The glorious ensign of Emmanuel's kingdom, once again established in the world, must be unfurled in every nation, kingdom, and empire: the voice of warning—the voice of the Bridegroom, "Prepare ye, prepare ye the way of the Lord," must be carried forth unto all people. You are the ones whom the Lord has chosen for this purpose, even the horn of Joseph, to "push the people together." Surely you cannot be too anxiously, nor too industriously engaged, seeking how best, the manner most useful to yourselves and mankind, to magnify your holy and sacred offices. (1 December 1851, MS, 13:362; BLS, p. 192.)

Gospel conversations should be conducted in the right spirit. The Savior has commanded not to cast pearls before swine. I am sorry to say that this instruction is not always sufficiently re-garded by those to whom our Lord has given, through the ever-lasting covenant, His pearls of wisdom, knowledge, and precious gifts. The consequence is, we lose blessings instead of retaining them—a decrease of the Holy Spirit follows, instead of an in-crease, and our minds become darkened.

What I allude to is this: we too frequently engage in conver-sation concerning things of the kingdom of God, with persons of a wrong spirit; and feeling overanxious to make them see, under-stand and acknowledge the light presented, we urge on, and per-sist in the conversation until we partake of the spirit of those with whom we are conversing. We ought to be particularly guarded against falling into errors of this kind.

It is very easy to understand when conversation is attended with profit. We then feel our minds enlightened, and the power of God resting upon us through the Holy Spirit—ideas flow into our minds, and we express them with ease, freedom, and calm-ness.

Conversation conducted in this spirit proves highly profit-able, not only to ourselves, but also to those with whom we converse; and after its close, our hearts are drawn out in gratitude to the Most High for the privilege of imparting the glorious truths of the gospel to the children of men. (13 May 1841, BLS, p. 59.)

CHAPTER 11

Priesthood: Honoring the Power of God

Magnifying priesthood callings requires our highest efforts. In building up the kingdom of God, which is the work assigned us, our whole attention and highest efforts are demanded, that we may be qualified, through the Holy Spirit, to properly magnify our respective callings in the holy priesthood. (7 October 1873, JD, 16:273.)

The priesthood is the channel for exaltation. There is a certain channel by and through which the Lord intends to exalt His sons and daughters, to remove wickedness from the earth and to establish righteousness, and that channel is the priesthood, which God has established and shown clearly the nature and character of the various officers and duties thereof. The Apostles and the Seventies, it is their business by the appointment of the Almighty, to look after the interests of the world. The Seventies and the Twelve Apostles are special witnesses unto the nations of the earth. The business of the high priests, the elders and the bishops is to look after the interests of these various organizations that I have mentioned. (6 October 1901, CR, p. 61.)

Men must administer salvation to continue in the priesthood. Men who wish to retain their standing before God in the holy priesthood must have the spirit of prophecy, and be qualified to administer life and salvation to the people; and if they cannot do it to the world, they must do it at home, in their families, in their shops, and in the streets, that their hearts may be inspired with words of life at their firesides, in teaching the gospel to their children and to their neighbors. (4 January 1857, JD, 4:157.)

The priesthood is given to bring happiness. The object of the priesthood is to make all men happy, to diffuse information, to make all partakers of the same blessings in their turn. (7 April 1861, JD, 9:22.)

Who would dishonor his priesthood? And now, where is the man among you [who], having once burst the veil and gazed upon this purity, the glory, the might, majesty and dominion of a perfected man, in celestial glory, in eternity, will not cheerfully resign mortal life—suffer most excruciating tortures—let limb be torn from limb, sooner than dishonor or resign his priesthood. (1 December 1851, MS, 13:363; BLS, p. 195.)

We should honor our callings. I remember reading an anecdote when a boy of a man who, through his wisdom and patriotism, had gained great renown, but who through envy was assigned to a position which was considered very degrading. On entering upon its duties it was said that he made this significant remark: "If the office does not honor me I will honor the office." Much difficulty would be avoided, and our condition and situation would be much more encouraging if we all honored the office in which we are called to act. We are told that the Lord himself made clothes for our first parents, or, in other words, on that occasion, acted as tailor; also that Jesus Christ was a carpenter. Now the Savior must have been an honorable and honest carpenter or he never could have merited the position he afterwards occupied. If we could get the brethren and sisters to see the importance of acting honestly and faithfully in their respective callings, much of the annoyances and troubles we now experience would be averted, and the work of God would roll on with redoubled rapidity, and all His purposes would be more rapidly and speedily accomplished; and besides, as a people, we would be better prepared than we now are for the dispensation of His will. (31 January 1877, DN, 25:834.)

The Lord chooses humble men. The Lord has not chosen the great and learned of the world to perform His work on the earth. It is not those who have been trained and educated in the colleges and seminaries of learning, but humble men devoted to His cause whom He has chosen to take charge of the affairs of His Church, men who are willing to be led and guided by the Holy Spirit, and who will of necessity give the glory unto Him knowing that of themselves they can do nothing. (8 October 1898, DW, 57:513.)

Priesthood holders are to qualify for the Spirit. High priests, seventies, and ye elders of Israel, are you this day prepared with wisdom and power to officiate for the living and the dead, and to lay a pure and holy foundation through your wives and children, that salvation may go forth to the rising generations? Or have you neglected qualifying yourselves in your holy callings, and let the cares of the world occupy your entire thoughts and attention, and your minds become dull, your spiritual armor rusty and but little room found in you for the Holy Ghost to abide?

Brethren, your eye should be single to the glory of God, to harkening to the counsel of the living prophet and to the building up of Zion; then your bodies would be filled with spirit, and your understandings with light, and your hearts with joy, and your souls would be quickened into eternal life with the power of the Holy Ghost. You would then become the depositories of that wisdom and knowledge which would qualify you to be saviors unto your brethren and your posterity. (4 January 1857, JD, 4:154-55.)

Proper use of the priesthood leads to eternal glory. To my brethren in the priesthood I beg to offer a few words of counsel, instruction, and exhortation. Upon you rest high and sacred responsibilities, which relate not only to the salvation of this generation, but of many past generations, and many to come. The glorious ensign of Emmanuel's kingdom, once again established in the world, must be unfurled in every nation, kingdom, and empire: the voice of warning—the voice of the Bridegroom, "Prepare ye, prepare ye the way of the Lord," must be carried forth unto all people. You are the ones whom the Lord has chosen for this purpose, even the horn of Joseph, to "push the people together." Surely you cannot be too anxiously, nor too industriously engaged, seeking how best, the manner most useful to yourselves and mankind, to magnify your holy and sacred offices.

It is the priesthood that will give you character, renown, wisdom, power, and authority, and build you up here below among the children of men; and above, exalt you to peace and happiness, to glory, to thrones and dominions, even through countless eternities. This world, in its kingdoms and empires, possesses, in some degree, glory and greatness, faintly shadowing forth what is embraced in regions above; but here, to these, is joined little happiness, little durability.

The world we seek offers to its inhabitants unfading glory, immortal renown, and dominions of continued increase, where families grow into nations, nations into generations, generations into worlds, worlds into universes: this is *the path* of the priesthood—*the path* of the Holy Ones. Well did the Apostle say, "Eye hath not seen, nor ear heard, neither hath it entered into the heart of man to conceive the things that God hath prepared for them that love Him, but God hath revealed them unto us by His Spirit, for the Spirit searcheth all things, yea, even the deep things of God."

Authoritative rule is not the proper rule by which to govern Saints, but rather seek to administer in the spirit of humility, wisdom, and goodness, teaching not so much by theory as by practice. Though one teach with the eloquence of an angel, yet one's good practice, good examples, one's acts constantly manifesting whole-heartedness for the interests of the people, teach much more eloquently, much more effectually. Very few indeed have enough moral courage to be strictly honest, faithful, virtuous, and honorable in all positions—these few will hold the priesthood and receive its fulness, but no others.

Purity, virtue, fidelity, and godliness must be sought ambitiously, or the crown cannot be won. Those principles must be incorporated with[in] ourselves—woven into our constitutions—becoming a part of us, making us a center, a fountain of truth, of equity, justice, and mercy, of all that is good and great; that from us may proceed the light, the life, the power, and the law to direct, to govern, and assist to save a wandering world—acting as the sons of God, for and in behalf of our Father in heaven. We expect, in the Resurrection, to exercise the powers of our priesthood—we can exercise them only in proportion as we secure its righteousness and perfection. These qualifications can be had only as they are sought and obtained; so that in the morning of the Resurrection we will possess those acquisitions only which we secured in this world! Godliness cannot be conferred, but must be acquired—a fact of which the religious world seems strangely and lamentably unconscious.

Seek to benefit others, and others will seek to benefit you—he that would be great, let him be good, studying the interests of the whole—becoming the servant of all, whereby he will secure to himself most of the wisdom and power of God, the love, esteem, and veneration of His people.

The elders must become persons of the highest responsibility. The happiness of people, nations, and of generations, will depend upon the right and faithful exercise of the powers of their offices. If, in a lesser sphere of action, they fail to be trustworthy, who will depend upon them in the greater? In view of the vast responsibilities to be placed upon men in this high calling, they are in a measure left to themselves, to act upon their agency. If they pass onward to the close of this probation, without being overthrown by evil powers, keeping their spirits pure, and, through the power of the Holy Ghost, educate and build themselves up in those qualifications essential to such exaltations, then in due time God will elevate them to those positions. (1 December 1851, MS, 13:362-63; BLS, pp. 192-94.)

A priesthood holder should be faithful regardless of his calling. Now the question is, do we sense our position, do we comprehend fully the nature of the work we have undertaken to consummate? I am sometimes led to believe that some of our brethren, elders in Israel, are too ready and willing to shirk to obligations they are under by reason of their covenants, the faith they once possessed seems to be almost exhausted, and they appear to settle down into the quiet satisfaction of a mere nominal membership in the Church. There are others who think because their names are not very widely known, because they are perhaps only employees, occupying narrow spheres, that it does not matter much what habits they contract, or what kind of examples they set before their brethren. But then, if they held responsible positions, such as the Presidency of the Church, or a counselorship, or if they belonged to the Quorum of the Twelve, or were they president of the high council, or of the high priests or seventies, then they would consider it important how they conducted themselves. Herein they manifest great weakness or gross ignorance, their lamp is either growing dim or they never sensed the position they assumed in taking upon themselves the responsibilities of the gospel. (6 October 1876, JD, 18:299.)

We are told in the parable of the Savior that the kingdom of heaven is as a householder who delivered his goods to his servants as he was about to travel into a far country. To one he gave five talents, to another two, and to another one. The one that received the five talents went and traded, and made other five talents, doubling the portion that had been entrusted to him, and he also that received two talents went and gained other two. But he that received the one talent, went and digged in the earth, and hid his lord's money. He doubtless considered that his responsibility was so small that he could not do much, and consequently he would not exercise a talent so inferior. Does not this apply directly to the condition of some of our elders? Says one, "I am only a carpenter, or a tailor, or peradventure only a hod-carrier, therefore it cannot matter much how I deport myself, whether I do or do not honestly discharge my duties in my humble sphere. But it would be very different if I were acting in some more responsible and prominent position."

Stop, my brother; do not allow yourself to be deceived by such alluring sentiments. It is true you may only be a hod carrier, but remember you are an elder in Israel, you are an ambassador of the Lord Jesus Christ, and if you are in the line of your duty you are in possession of that which the world cannot give nor take away; and you are held accountable to God for the honest use of the talent over which he has made you steward, whether it be large or small.

Therefore, let it be understood and always remembered by those who may be called to follow the humbler occupations in life, that it is absolutely necessary, for their growth and progress in the kingdom of God, that while acting therein they master the situation, that they establish and form a character and a living name by which they may be known and distinguished hereafter among the sons of God. I respect the man occupying the humblest position, if he is faithful in the sphere in which he acts, and is truly an honest man; I deem him just as honorable as any person who may act in a higher position. The Lord does not require so much of the man who possesses but one talent, as of him who possesses more than one; but, according to that which he hath, so shall it be required of him. Let all, therefore, be encouraged, and seek to improve the talents they severally possess; and let him who may have the one talent use it and not hide it in the earth; that is, let him who may be endowed with little ability improve himself, and not complain because nature may not have been so propitious to him as to his more fortunate brother. Let us all be satisfied with our lot in life, and should it not be so desirable as we could wish, we should seek with becoming diligence to improve it, ever feeling grateful for our earthly being, and more especially for the Spirit of God we have received through obedience to the gospel. (31 January 1877, DN, 25:834.)

Priesthood leaders are to feed the Lord's sheep. I will now say, let every man who stands in an official station, on whom God has bestowed His holy and divine priesthood, think of what the Savior said to the Twelve Apostles just before He went into the presence of His Father: "Feed my sheep." And He continued to say this until His Apostles felt sorrowful that he should continue to call upon them in this manner. But, said He, "Feed my sheep." That is, "Go forth with your whole heart, be devoted wholly to my cause. These people in the world are my brethren and sisters. My feelings are exercised towards them. Take care of my people. Feed my flock. Go forth and preach the gospel. I will reward you for all your sacrifices. Do not think that you can make too great a sacrifice in accomplishing this work." He called upon them in the fervor of His heart to do this work.

And now I call upon all who hold this priesthood, the presiding officers of this stake, and the bishops, and the high council, to go forth and feed the flock. Take an interest in them. Did you ever lose a child, and the parting struck keenly into your souls? Transfer a little of this deep feeling to the interests of the Saints over whom you are called to preside, and in whose interests you have received the holy priesthood. Work for them, and do not confine your thoughts and feelings to your personal aggrandizement. Then God will give you revelation, inspiration upon inspiration, and teach you how to secure the interests of the Saints in matters pertaining to their temporal and spiritual welfare. (19 October 1879, JD, 20:372.)

Stake presidents should look after the Saints under their charge. This church is now nearly seventy-two years of age, and we are not expected to do the work of the days of our youth, but to do greater, larger, and more extensive work. The Lord is coming one of these days, and He is interested in the work that you ought to be doing and anxious to be doing. You ought to do all that you possibly can, and leave everything in your business affairs that you wisely can do and attend to these matters. The presidents of these fifty stakes should consider the people in their respective stakes, in their various dominions. They should regard them as their own family, as their sons and daughters; and take as deep an interest in them as they ought to take in their own wives and children. It should be their thought by day and by night, how and in what way they can be most serviceable to their respective charges. Oh! brethren, do remember these things that I am now talking about; do not forget them. You presidents, when you retire to your rest, you probably can spend half an hour before you go to sleep, and let your thoughts run over your several jurisdictions. See wherein, either physically, financially, or spiritually, you can help, and what can be done best in advancing the interests of your official family. These bishops, however wise and energetic they may think themselves—and the most of them certainly are very wise and energetic—need to be looked after. It is not the duty of the Apostles to look after them. (6 October 1901, CR, pp. 60-61.)

Local Church leaders should take initiative in reforming the Saints. I wanted to say this, and to speak it with energy and in a way that you will not forget it, that you cannot forget it. It is a wonderful responsibility, and the Lord expects it of you. You ought to know how the laws of God are observed in your respective localities—how the Sabbath is kept; whether the young people are swearing, and off at midnight when they ought to be at home; how the parents govern and control them; how far the people are paying their tithing correctly; what they are doing in regard to their meetinghouses, their schoolhouses, and their houses of amusement; whether they are expending their time and means too much in these directions, or not enough; and what you can do in helping them along. Look at these things, and everything that pertains to the happiness of your children, the members of this family of yours, see what you can do about it. And the Lord God of Israel will help you in this, because it is just what He wants you to do. It is the duty that He has placed upon you to discharge, and He certainly will help you. But when you take any other course—when you depend upon the Apostles to reform your respective stakes—you are doing that which you have no business to do. Do it yourselves, you presidents of stakes and counselors, you high councilors, and you bishops. (6 October 1901, CR, p. 61.)

There are greater things than being an Apostle. It is a great thing, we say, for a man to be an Apostle; yet there are things you can look forward to which are greater than this. A man has no reason to envy his friend because he happens to get a little higher than himself. The glory that is before us is open to every man and every woman, through this gospel, which is the power of God unto salvation, glory, and exaltation in the fulness thereof. (9 October 1898, CR, p. 56.)

An Apostle must possess divine knowledge and authority. It becomes proper for me to explain some essential qualifications of an Apostle.

First, an Apostle must possess a divine knowledge, by revelation from God, that Jesus lives—that He is the Son of the living God.

Secondly, he must be divinely authorized to promise the Holy Ghost; a divine principle that reveals the things of God, making known His will and purposes, leading into all truth, and showing things to come, as declared by the Savior.

Thirdly, he is commissioned by the power of God to administer the sacred ordinances of the gospel, which are confirmed to each individual by a divine testimony. Thousands of people now dwelling in these mountain vales, who received these ordinances through my administrations, are living witnesses of the truth of this statement. (15 February 1886, MS, 48:110.)

The priesthood is the channel for knowledge and salvation. The priesthood or authority in which we stand is the medium or channel through which our Heavenly Father has purposed to communicate light, intelligence, gifts, powers, and spiritual and temporal salvation unto the present generation. (May, 1841, MS, 2:39.)

CHAPTER 12

Following the Brethren

Follow the Brethren and all will be well. If you will be as faithful and united as the First Presidency and Twelve are faithful and united, and will follow us as we follow Christ, all will be well with you. We are determined to perform our duty and to serve the Lord and labor for the benefit of His people and the accomplishment of His work. We are your servants in the Lord and desire your welfare and the welfare of all mankind. (8 October 1898, DW, 57:513.)

Follow the living prophet. The people are under obligation to obey the counsel that is given; they are necessarily required to apply the counsel of the living prophet, because that counsel possesses those objects. No man can be more happy than by obeying the living prophet's counsel. You may go from east to west, from north to south, and tread this footstool of the Lord all over, and you cannot find a man that can make himself happy in this Church, only by applying the counsel of the living prophet in this life; it is a matter of impossibility for a man to receive a fulness who is not susceptible of receiving and carrying out the living prophet's counsel. An individual that applies the counsel of this Church is bound to increase in all that is good, for there is a fountain of counsel which the Lord has established. He has made it, has deposited that counsel, that wisdom and those riches, and it will circumscribe all that pertains unto good, unto salvation; all that pertains unto peace and unto happiness; all things that pertain to glory and to the exaltation of the Saints in this world and in the world to come. (18 January 1857, JD, 4:184.)

Following the prophet brings safety. When the enemy is near, and when the stormy clouds arise, and the war clouds approach, even then we can feel free and quiet, and be satisfied that all is right in Israel. It is only for us to be ready to do our duty, to serve our President with all our heart, with all our might, with all our feelings, with all our property and energies, and with all things that the Lord has put into our hands. (11 October 1857, JD, 5:314.)

The Spirit teaches us to follow the Brethren. The Holy Spirit of light, that brings intelligence to us and an understanding of sacred things, belongs to every member of the Church. They have a right to pass their opinion upon those that are presiding over them. The works and the labors that the officers perform in the presence of this people may be known and understood by every member of the Church—in a general way, at least. There may be some things that the First Presidency do, that the Apostles do, that cannot for the moment be explained; yet the spirit, the motives that inspire the action can be understood, because each member of the Church has a right to have that measure of the Spirit of God that they can judge as to those who are acting in their interests or otherwise. (9 October 1898, CR, p. 54.)

We should honor the callings of priesthood holders. Here are brethren before and around us in this congregation who have received from God a holy, sacred priesthood, to minister in His name. Divine authority and appointment was given Saul, which David regarded so sacredly that he did not dare to raise his hand against him, although a mortal enemy and one who was preventing him from ascending the throne that God had given him. How do we regard these our brethren—their sacred appointments? David would not even allow his servant to touch Saul.

He was not like the Quaker of whom I heard when I was a boy. He had a dog which displeased him. Now, the Quakers do not believe in killing anybody, not even a serpent. This Quaker wished to stand by his principles, but he wanted to get rid of this dog. So he turned him out in the streets, and called out so that everybody could hear, "Mad dog, mad dog." The result was the people stoned the dog to death.

There was something grand in this trait of character which David exhibited on that occasion as well as on many others. How do we feel under such circumstances? How do we feel sometimes in regard to our friends and neighbors who hold the holy priesthood? Do we slander them, and call "Mad dog, mad dog," so that others will slander them also? Or do we seek to sustain them as our brethren? Do we try to ascertain their faults and weaknesses, or do we try to ascertain their good qualities? Do we regard as sacred that priesthood and that authority which they hold, as David did in the case of Saul? Or is it otherwise with us? (6 May 1889, DW, 38:763.)

Raising a hand is not enough in sustaining our leaders. It is an easy thing for us to rise here and raise our right hands in token of our approval of what is presented before us. I can do that without any trouble, and so can you. But there is something involved in this rising here and raising our right hands in approval of the propositions presented; there is a meaning to it; something that ought to be well considered, and that is, acting in the future in accordance with this manifestation of our approval. Now, I know—and I know it well; nobody can know it better—that if this mighty priesthood and these Latter-day Saints that are before me will act up to that which they have approved by raising their right hands and in accordance with the motives that undoubtedly inspired them, the progress of this Church will be more rapid than it has been in the past. (9 October 1898, CR, p. 54.)

The purpose of our leaders' counsel is to bring happiness. Counsel that is given to us, when it comes from the proper authority, is given for a certain purpose; and that purpose is our happiness, so far as the present time is concerned; it is for the purpose of adding happiness unto us in the present state, and also for the purpose of communicating benefits unto us in a state hereafter. Upon this principle is counsel established, upon the principle of doing our fellowmen good; for the purpose of doing them good here and hereafter. (18 January 1857, JD, 4:183.)

Follow your local leaders. It requires more energy and more strength of purpose in a man to follow out the counsel of one who is just above him than it does to follow a man that is a long way ahead of him. (11 October 1857, JD, 5:315.)

Wise counsel benefits the giver. No man can give counsel to anyone, but what it has a tendency to benefit himself as well as others. We are so constituted and organized, that we cannot counsel that which will contribute to the benefit and exaltation of others without at the same time contributing to our own good. (18 January 1857, JD, 4:184.)

Pray for the Brethren at conference time. When the Brethren arise to speak you should ask the Lord to let them say something that you want to know, that they may suggest something to you that will be of some advantage. If you have any desire to know certain matters that you do not understand, pray that these brethren in their talks may say something that shall enlighten your mind in reference to that which troubles you, and we will have a grand and glorious conference, a better one than we have ever had before. Strange as it may appear, our last conference always seems the best, and may this be the case; and you brethren and sisters, let your hearts rise up to the Lord and exercise faith while our brethren are talking to you. We will not be disappointed, and you will not go home, you will not retire from this conference, without feeling you have been greatly and abundantly blessed. (5 October 1900, CR, p. 5.)

We assemble to learn the will of God. On occasions of this kind, when we are assembled together to learn the will of God, it is of importance that we exercise faith, and have the spirit of prayer, that the Lord will cause something to be said that will instruct, and give us such information and knowledge as will be of use and service in our daily walk and under the circumstances that surround us. (21 April 1878, JD, 19:341.)

Our being edified at conference depends on us. It becomes necessary that we prepare our hearts to receive and profit by the suggestions that may be made by the speakers during the progress of the conference, which may be prompted by the Spirit of the Lord. I have thought, and still think, that our being edified does not so much depend upon the speaker as upon ourselves. (6 October 1898, CR, p. 1.)

We should pay attention at conference. At these general conferences it is the privilege of everyone who attends to receive instruction, suited to his individual needs and benefits, of great worth, and if we pay proper attention to what is said and exercise the proper faith, there will be no disappointment. (5 October 1897, CR, p. 29.)

The message matters most, not the style of oratory. I have noticed on the part of the people what I have attributed to weakness. They come together, some of them, more for the purpose of being pleased with the oratory of their speaker, for the purpose of admiring the style in which he may address them, or they come together more for the purpose of seeing the speaker or speculating in regard to his character, or the true relationship that he sustains to the Lord in the priesthood, than for the purpose of receiving instructions that will do them good and build them up in righteousness. (18 January 1857, JD, 4:182.)

CHAPTER 13

The Plan of Salvation

God's plan is for universal salvation. God loves His offspring, the human family. His design is not simply to furnish happiness to the few here, called Latter-day Saints. The plan and scheme that He is now carrying out is for universal salvation; not only for the salvation of the Latter-day Saints, but for the salvation of every man and woman on the face of the earth, for those also in the spirit world, and for those who may hereafter come upon the face of the earth. It is for the salvation of every son and daughter of Adam. They are the offspring of the Almighty, He loves them all and His plans are for the salvation of the whole, and He will bring all up into that position in which they will be as happy and as comfortable as they are willing to be. (14 January 1872, JD, 14:308.)

We made covenants in pre-earth life. I often ask myself, what am I in the world for? Where did I come from, and where am I going? Well, we have learned something in regard to this. We have learned that we existed with God in eternity before we came into this life, and that we kept our estate. Had we not kept what is called our first estate and observed the laws that governed there, you and I would not be here today. We are here because we are worthy to be here, and that arises, to a great extent at least, from the fact that we kept our first estate. I believe that when you and I were in yonder life we made certain covenants with those that had the control that in this life, when we should be permitted to enter it, we would do what we had done in that life—find out the will of God and conform to it. I have not the least idea that I would be here today talking to you, unless it was distinctly understood in that life that when I came into this I would be obedient to the will of God as it should be revealed. Of course, we have forgotten these things; but the Lord is beginning to illuminate our understandings and is bringing to our recollection certain things in regard to how we were there, and for what we have come into this world. What you and I now want to know is how to secure the position we occupied in the other life when we go back, and that which will naturally be added to us in consequence of the experience that we had in this life; for the Lord has told us that those who would keep their second estate, glory should be added upon their heads forever and ever. It seems to me that no man or woman can afford to do anything in this life only that which, directly or indirectly, will be in conformity to the will of God. (12 May 1894, DW, 48:637.)

We chose to be on earth. We are in the world for a purpose. We are not here accidentally. We came here because we were willing to come, and because it was the wish of our Father in Heaven that we should come. We undoubtedly saw very clearly that there was no other way for us to secure what the Father had in store for us. (5 April 1901, CR, p. 2.)

Some did not keep their first estate. We came into this world because we kept our first estate in the midst of all the trials and difficulties in the other life. It was not all of the family of God that preserved themselves in their first estate. One-third part of the host of the children of God, His offspring, traveled in a different direction, and were not worthy to come into the world. (1 June 1895, DW, 50:738.)

Life's difficulties were known in premortal life. I dare say that in the spirit world, when it was proposed to us to come into this probation, and pass through the experience that we are now receiving, it was not altogether pleasant and agreeable; the prospects were not so delightful in all respects as might have been desired. Yet there is no doubt that we saw and understood clearly there that, in order to accomplish our exaltation and glory, this was a necessary experience; and however disagreeable it might have appeared to us, we were willing to conform to the will of God, and consequently we are here. (4 November 1893, DW, 47:609.)

Pre-earth life affects relations here. We have not come into this world accidentally. It is my opinion that there has been an inspiration to bring about certain relations that we are forming here in this life, and most likely they arise because of certain relations that existed in our previous life. (1 June 1895, DW, 50:737.)

The Saints have special missions here. Now, there are several thousand Latter-day Saints before me, and there is not one but has a work to perform. We did not come into this world accidentally. We came for a special purpose, and it was undoubtedly through certain arrangements in the other life where we dwelt that we came into this life. (1 June 1895, DW, 50:737.)

The Lord will test the Saints. The Latter-day Saints have done wonders; but they cannot cease from doing wonders in the future. There will be greater things demanded of the Latter-day Saints than have ever been demanded since the organization of the Church. The Lord has determined in His heart that He will try us until He knows what He can do with us. He tried His Son Jesus. Thousands of years before He came upon earth, the Father had watched His course and knew that He could depend upon Him when the salvation of worlds should be at stake; and He was not disappointed. So in regard to ourselves. He will try us, and continue to try us, in order that He may place us in the highest positions in life and put upon us the most sacred responsibilities. (18 May 1899, MS, 61:532.)

Earth life is necessary to prepare us for exaltation. Circumstances were of that nature that men and women never could be exalted and receive the fulness of glory unless they passed through this ordeal. They had to come to the earth, which was called the second estate. We had a first estate, in which we dwelt, moved, and had a being. We knew one another there. And in consequence of having kept our first estate, we had the privilege of coming unto this estate, in order to pass through the ordeal and get that necessary experience and education that should prepare us to sit upon thrones and govern and control our posterity worlds without end. We came here because we were sent here and because we were willing to come. (1 June 1895, DW, 50:737.)

We should desire to live long upon the earth. Among us, I am happy to say, old age is honorable, and regarded as a blessing from the Lord. It is our duty to desire to live long upon the earth, that we may do as much good as we possibly can. I esteem it a great privilege to have the opportunity of living in mortality. The Lord has sent us here "for a wise and glorious purpose," and it should be our business to find out what that purpose is and then to order our lives accordingly. (2 July 1901, JH, p. 5.)

Our identity will always remain the same. In considering ourselves and how we have been organized and what we are doing, we discover that there is immortality connected with us. We are immortal beings. That which dwells in this body of ours is immortal, and will always exist. Our individuality will always continue. Eternities may begin, eternities may end, and still we shall have our individuality. Our identity is insured. We will be ourselves and nobody else. Whatever changes may arise, whatever worlds may be made or pass away, our identity will always remain the same; and we will continue on improving, advancing, and increasing in wisdom, intelligence, power, and dominion, worlds without end. Our present advancement is simply a starting out, as it were, on this path of immortality. Whatever may have been our past, how long we may have existed before this, or whether there ever was a time when we did not exist, there is one thing sure—our being in the future will never be annihilated, never destroyed. (5 April 1901, CR, p. 2.)

We must progress or lose what we have. We should labor for perfection so far as possible, and seek to go onward. There is no man or woman who can stand still any great length of time. In this path over which we are moving we are very likely to go backward if we undertake to stand still or act indifferently. We must push forward, because as the Church moves on, it is very evident that things of a more difficult character are occurring constantly, and we will find it far from easy to overcome them. Unless we improve as we move along we will find it very difficult to magnify our callings and to perform the work required at our hands. Latter-day Saints should not permit themselves to stand still. It is a privilege we have to serve the Lord and enjoy His spirit in our labors, but many of the people lose that portion of happiness that they might enjoy because of not reflecting seriously upon their duties and acting wisely and prudently. (6 April 1898, CR, p. 12.)

We must work for our own exaltation. I cannot imagine anything that is so vastly important as to work for and obtain one's own individual exaltation and glory. That undoubtedly is one great purpose for which we came into the world. When we lived in the other life we had no doubt some understanding with reference to our duties in this life when we were permitted to come to this our second estate. And very likely we put ourselves under certain obligations that we would discharge certain duties devolving upon us when we came here into our second estate. And we had rendered ourselves worthy to come upon this earth for the purpose of securing those blessings that could only be obtained by observing the laws pertaining to our present estate. (6 April 1898, CR, p. 12.)

Infant baptism is unnecessary. Faith and repentance go before baptism, and baptism before the remission of sins and the re-

ception of the Holy Ghost. Hence, we see the useless and un-
scriptural practice of baptizing infants. They cannot exercise
faith and repentance, qualifications necessary previous to baptism; then why require the outward work? (1841, SML, p. 78.)

Temple work is the most important work. We feel when we
go into these temples that we enjoy the Spirit of the Lord more
fully than in any other place. They are the Lord's buildings, and
His most important work is carried on within their walls. We are
satisfied—at least I am, and I believe many of the brethren look
upon it in the same light—that the most important work that
Latter-day Saints can do on this earth is that of opening the door
for the salvation of their kindred dead. There is but one way in
which men can receive salvation, exaltation, and glory, and that
is through the order of baptism and the ordinances connected
therewith. No mortal man or woman will ever receive celestial
glory unless he or she has been baptized, receiving this ordinance
personally or by proxy. That is the order that God has established. (3 April 1897, DW, 54:482.)

Temples are places for us to be taught and prepared. It looks
to me now, the way things are moving, that our temples are the
grand places where people will be taught and prepared for the
things they will have to endure in the not far distant future. (3
April 1897, DW, 54:482.)

Temple work is essential to salvation. Now, in our temples we
allow persons to come in, after they have traced their ancestry, no
matter how far back, and to be baptized for their dead father,
grandfather, and great grandfather and so on, just as far as they
can trace their line. Then we allow them to have the wives sealed
to their husbands all along the ancestry line, as far as they can
trace it. Take the case of a virtuous young man who lived before
the gospel was introduced to the children of men. He desired to
get him a wife and to raise a family. That desire is a proper desire.

It is obeying the first commandment. Well, he married a wife, and he raised a family; but he never had the privilege of receiving the gospel, as you and I have. However, he taught his family the principles of morality, and was affectionate and kind to his wife and children. What more could he do? He should not be condemned because he did not receive the gospel; for there was no gospel to receive. He should not lose his wife because when he married her he could not go into a temple and have her sealed to him for time and eternity. He acted according to the best knowledge that he had, and she was married to him for time.

When we go back into the other life and find our dead friends living there, if we have not performed the labor that is necessary for their exaltation and glory we shall not feel very happy and it will not be a very pleasant meeting. We ought not to wait for opportunities to be pleasant and agreeable always; but we should strive, even if it takes a little sacrifice on our part, to put ourselves in a condition to perform this labor.

We welcome the brethren and sisters when we see them in this temple. It is the same in all the other temples. We desire anxiously that the brethren and sisters should not neglect this important work. Do you know what will be the main labor during the thousand years of rest? It will be that which we are trying to urge the Latter-day Saints to perform at the present time. Temples will be built all over this land, and the brethren and sisters will go into them and perhaps work day and night in order to hasten the work and accomplish the labors necessary before the Son of Man can present His kingdom to His Father. This work has got to be accomplished before the Son of Man can come and receive His kingdom to present it to His Father. Every son and daughter of God will have the opportunity necessary for exaltation and glory, either by themselves or by their friends. For there is but one way by which exaltation and glory can be secured. We have to be baptized for the remission of sins and have hands laid upon us for the reception of the Holy Ghost. These and other ordinances are absolutely necessary for exaltation and glory; and where individuals have lived when the gospel has not been accessible, these things can be attended to by their friends. We have come into the world now in order to do these things—at least, it is one of the chief objects of our coming. We cannot lay too great stress upon the importance of this work. (1 June 1895, DW, 50:738.)

It was difficult for Jesus to accomplish the Atonement. Jesus, the Son of God, was sent into the world to make it possible for you and me to receive these extraordinary blessings. He had to make a great sacrifice. It required all the power that He had and all the faith that He could summon for Him to accomplish that which the Father required of Him. Had He fallen in the moment of temptation, what do you suppose would have become of us? Doubtless at some future period the plan would have been carried out by another person. But He did not fail, though the trial was so severe that He sweat great drops of blood. When He knelt there in the Garden of Gethsemane, what agony He must have experienced in contemplating His sufferings on the cross! His feelings must have been inexpressible. He tells us Himself, as you will find recorded in section 19 of the book of Doctrine and Covenants, that His suffering was so great that it caused even Him "to tremble because of pain, and to bleed at every pore, and to suffer both body and spirit—and would that [He] might not drink the bitter cup, and shrink." But He had in His heart continually to say, "Father, not my will, but Thine be done." It was a dark hour for Him; and every man and woman who serves the Lord, no matter how faithful they may be, have their dark hours; but if they have lived faithfully, light will burst upon them and relief will be furnished. (18 May 1899, MS, 61:531.)

Missionary work is more successful in spirit prison than on earth. A wonderful work is being accomplished in our temples in favor of the spirits in prison. I believe, strongly too, that when the gospel is preached to the spirits in prison, the success attending that preaching will be far greater than that attending the preaching of our elders in this life. (4 November 1893, DW, 47:609.)

All will eventually accept the gospel. The antediluvians rejected the word of God; but they were the sons and daughters of God, and He did not reject them, only for a time. After twenty-five hundred years had passed away the Lord revealed Himself to them again and gave them another opportunity. Then they no doubt accepted, generally if not altogether, that which they refused in the days of Noah. The people of this generation may not receive our testimony here, but they will receive it at some future time, from us or from some other servants of God. (5 April 1901, CR, p. 3.)

Bishops and stake presidents are sentinels to guard the temples. The bishops and presidents of stakes should stand as sentinels, and they should not allow any to pass by them into the temple that are unworthy. It is something like what we learn in the temple about a time that is coming when persons who go into the celestial kingdom will have to pass by the angels and the gods. (3 April 1897, DW, 54:482.)

Nothing is more beautiful than a resurrected being. We know that in the future, after we have passed through this life, we will then have our wives and our children with us. We will have our bodies glorified, made free from every sickness and distress, and rendered most beautiful. There is nothing more beautiful to look upon than a resurrected man or woman. There is nothing grander that I can imagine that a man can possess than a resurrected body. There is no Latter-day Saint within the sound of my voice but that certainly has this prospect of coming forth in the morning of the First Resurrection and being glorified, exalted in the presence of God, having the privilege of talking with our Father as we talk with our earthly father. (5 October 1900, CR, p. 4.)

The faithful will stand before multitudes of their own posterity. You who are seated here will have opportunities of standing in the presence of multitudes, and I can easily imagine, yonder in the next life, after we have passed along perhaps a thousand years or more, that many of you who are here today will have an audience before you of your own posterity. I am as sure of it as I am that I am talking to you; I know it just as well as I know anything. (9 October 1898, CR, p. 55.)

"Mormonism" is the original plan of salvation. Mormonism, a nickname for the real religion of the Latter-day Saints, does not profess to be a new thing, except to this generation. It proclaims itself as the original plan of salvation, instituted in the heavens before the world was, and revealed from God to man in different ages. That Adam, Enoch, Noah, Abraham, Moses, and other ancient worthies had this religion successively, in a series of dispensations, we, as a people, verily believe. To us, the gospel taught by the Redeemer in the meridian of time was a restored gospel, of which, however, He was the author, in His pre-existent state. Mormonism, in short, is the primitive Christian faith restored, the ancient gospel brought back again—this time to usher in the last dispensation, introduce the Millennium, and wind up the work of redemption as pertaining to this planet. (2 January 1902, MS, 64:1-2.)

We control our destiny. The ultimatum of our travel in this path of exaltation will bring to us the fulness of our Lord Jesus Christ, to stand in the presence of our Father, to receive of His fulness, to have the pleasure of increasing in our posterity worlds without end, to enjoy those pleasant associations that we have had in this life, to have our sons and our daughters, our husbands and our wives, surrounded with all the enjoyment that heaven can bestow, our bodies glorified like unto the Savior's, free from disease and all the ills of life, and free from the disappointments and vexations and the unpleasant sacrifices that we are making here. We portray in our minds the glories that are before us, and we know that if we are faithful there will be no disappointment in the securing of these blessings. The power to prevent us from receiving these things is not in the hands of any man; it lies within ourselves. (18 May 1899, MS, 61:530.)

CHAPTER 14

Self-Control:
Overcoming Temptation

Learn to control your actions. In all your acts and conduct, ever have the consciousness that you are now preparing and making yourselves a life to be continued through eternities. Act upon no principle that you would be ashamed or unwilling to act upon in heaven—employ no means in the attainment of an object that an enlightened conscience disapproves. When feelings and passions excite you to action, let principles pure, honorable, and virtuous govern you. (1 December 1851, MS, 13:363.)

Self-denial preserves character. Our character, as Latter-day Saints, should be preserved inviolate, at whatever cost or sacrifice. Character approved of God is worth securing, even at the expense of a lifetime of constant self-denial.

While thus living we may look forward far away into the spiritland, with full assurance that when reaching that happy clime, we shall be crowned with the sons and daughters of God, and possess the wealth and glory of a celestial kingdom. (10 January 1886, JD, 26:368.)

We must learn to govern ourselves. We have received principles of truth, but not in blindness. We do not walk in blindness, but we walk in the light of truth. We know what we are about and what will be the result of our faithfulness. But we should be wise and prudent; we should learn to govern ourselves, to control our passions, and to bring all our faculties and powers into perfect obedience to the mind and will of God, so that these bodies, which God has given to us, may be governed and controlled in all respects as He would wish. (6 October 1899, CR, p. 2.)

Total devotion overcomes temptations. It is impossible for Latter-day Saints to move along in the path of glory we are now treading unless they devote themselves fully and wholly to the work and make the preparation which is absolutely necessary to meet and overcome the temptations that might otherwise overpower us. (6 October 1898, CR, p. 2.)

Withstand Satan. God admires the men and women today who pursue a course of rectitude and who, notwithstanding the powers of Satan that are arrayed against them, can say, Get thee behind me Satan, and who live a righteous, a godly life, and such people have influence with God and their prayers avail much. (6 May 1882, JD, 23:191.)

"Get behind me, Satan!" You may expect, if your lives are spared to the common age of man and womanhood, to encounter obstacles in the path of life which will test to the uttermost your best resolutions, and some of you may be tempted to swerve from the path of truth and honor, and, like Esau, feel to relinquish the glories of eternity for a few passing moments of gratification and pleasure; then, my dear children, seize your opportunity to emulate the example of our Savior when offered the glory of this world, if he would stoop to an act of folly; he replied to his tempter, "Get behind me, Satan!" (May 1884, BLS, p. 486.)

We must fortify ourselves against temptation. So soon as we discover ourselves in a fault, we should repent of that wrongdoing and as far as possible repair or make good the wrong we may have committed. By taking this course we strengthen our character, we advance our own cause, and we fortify ourselves against temptation. (6 May 1882, JD, 23:192.)

It is better to suffer a thousand deaths than to discard true principles. I wish to offer a word of caution to my brethren that you may beware, and commit no grave errors when brought into positions of trial and temptation. Some, unfortunately, have disregarded this injunction, and have imprinted a stain upon their character, and a blot upon their record which cannot be erased in time—perhaps not in eternity. These are fearful mistakes. Better suffer a thousand deaths than succumb to the force of persecution by promising to discard a single principle which God has revealed for our glory and exaltation. (10 January 1886, JD, 26:368.)

Some Church members are unfit for fellowship with the Saints. There are those among us who are recognized as members of this Church who take a vast amount of pains to be favorably known by those around them, but whose real character, or the inwardness, so to speak, of such people, is veiled or disguised, being to all outward appearance reputable Latter-day Saints, but whose inward character, the character that is written indelibly upon their own hearts, would, if known, render them unfit for the association and fellowship of the people of God. (6 May 1882, JD, 23:190.)

Greater temptations lie ahead, but the Saints will overcome. We are considerably advanced in the knowledge of the things of God, and are qualified to act in His behalf; yet we are not entirely out of the wilderness, if I may be permitted to use that expression. The time will come when we shall overcome the world and every temptation that can be advanced to affect us. We are now advancing to that point; but we have not yet reached it. And now comes a time when the Latter-day Saints will probably be subjected to temptation greater and more subtle than we ever again will experience as a people. But let me tell you that after we have passed through the scenes that are now before us, the clouds will break; and as President Woodruff has said, we will stand on a much higher plane of righteousness, of faith, power, and influence than ever before. We will have the approval and blessings of the Almighty, and we will have influence with the world. They will respect us more than they ever have done. (6 May 1889, DW, 38:763.)

Search me, O God. "Search me, O God, and know my heart . . . and see if there be any wicked way in me." (Psalm 139:23-24.) If we as a people could live so as to be able at all times to bow before the Lord and offer up a prayer like this, what a delightful thing it would be, what an attainment we should have acquired in righteousness and good works! To every person who has at heart the preparing of himself for the great change, that is the work of regeneration, I would recommend that he adopt this prayer of David, and see how near he can live according to the light that he has, so as to make it in all sincerity part of his devotions to God. Many fail in coming up to this standard of excellence because they do things in secret where mortal eye cannot penetrate, that has a direct tendency to alienate them from the Almighty, and to grieve away the Spirit of God. (6 May 1882, JD, 23:190.)

We should repent for the right reason. Undoubtedly it is too much the case with some that they consider and fear the publicity of the wrong they commit more than committing the wrong itself; they wonder what people will say when they hear of it. (6 May 1882, JD, 23:192.)

Repentance brings the Spirit. If you see that you have weaknesses which have brought you into some trouble, do not be discouraged; but repent of that which you have done wrong, by which you have lost more or less of the Spirit of God, tell the Lord what you have done, and resolve in your hearts that you will do it no more. Then the Spirit of the Lord will be upon you. (9 October 1898, CR, p. 56.)

We should govern ourselves wisely under all conditions.
Whatever may be the difficulties or the temptations that a person
may labor under, he should so govern and control himself that in
every condition he may act wisely and in a way that will increase
his intelligence, power, and faith. (9 October 1898, CR, p. 55.)

The Saints should prepare for the difficulties ahead. It is our
privilege as Latter-day Saints to seize upon those opportunities
that are afforded us to make a proper preparation for the scenes
that are before us and in which we may be called to act; and as
the difficulties which we have to meet shall increase upon us perhaps and become harder to overcome, we need more strength in
order to resist the temptations and to discharge the obligations
that devolve upon us. (10 April 1898, CR, pp. 61-62.)

CHAPTER 15

The Power of the Spirit

The Spirit of God and the Holy Ghost are not the same. There was a certain blessing connected only with obedience to the gospel, that was the gift of the Holy Ghost. When people received the ordinances of the gospel they were promised that they should receive the gift of the Holy Ghost. The Savior, who undoubtedly knew best about the nature and character of this gift, said it should lead all who received it into all truth and show them things to come. It should be more than that spirit which proceeds from God, filling the immensity of space and enlightening every man that comes into the world, the gift of the Holy Ghost should lead into all truth, and show them things to come. (14 January 1872, JD, 14:303.)

There is a great difference between the possession of the Holy Ghost and the mere possession of the Spirit of God. Everybody has the Spirit of God, that is, the honest-hearted, those who are living according to the best light they have. All Christian churches have it, those who seek truth and righteousness. The Baptists, if they are honest, have it; so have the Presbyterians and the Methodists; so also have all Christian and heathen nations. You go to China, and all honest-hearted people there have the Spirit of God; in fact we are told that this is the light that lights every man that comes into the world; but to say that all have the

Holy Ghost, the gift that was promised to those who obeyed the gospel, it is not so. (14 January 1872, JD, 14:304.)

People possess the Spirit of God in varying degrees. We believe that God is no respecter of persons, but that He confers blessings upon all His children in proportion to the light they have, or in proportion as they proceed according to the light and knowledge they possess in the different circumstances of life that may surround them. We believe that the spirit which enlightens the human family proceeds from the presence of the Almighty, that it spreads throughout all space, that it is the light and life of all things, and that every honest heart possesses it in proportion to his virtue, integrity, and his desire to know the truth and do good to his fellow men. (14 January 1872, JD, 14:300-301.)

The gift of the Holy Ghost is a principle of revelation. This gift of the Holy Ghost is a different principle from anything that we see manifested in the sectarian world. It is a principle of intelligence, and revelation. It is a principle that reveals things past, present, and to come, and these gifts of the Holy Ghost were to be received through obedience to the requirements of the gospel as proclaimed by the elders of the Church of Jesus Christ of Latter-day Saints in these days. (6 October 1879, JD, 20:330.)

We should seek the Spirit in every act. "As I hear, I judge: and my judgment is just; because I seek not mine own will, but the will of the Father which hath sent me" (John 5:30).

That is a wonderful saying, and there is a great deal in it. Now, what we want is to have that spirit in every act of our lives and in every undertaking, whether temporal or spiritual, and not think of self. We should try to ascertain how we should spend the money and the information that God has given us. The answer is simple—for the glory of God. Our eye should be single to the glory of God. That is what we have left the other life for and come into this. We should seek to promote the interests of the Most High God, and to feel as Jesus felt, "I can of mine own self do nothing." Inasmuch as we act today and tomorrow, this week and next week, in the interest of God, and have our eye single to His glory, there can be no failure. (12 May 1894, DW, 48:637.)

We need the Comforter. We need assistance. We are liable to do that which will lead us into trouble and darkness, and those things which will not tend to our good; but with the assistance of that Comforter which the Lord has promised His Saints, if we are careful to listen to its whisperings, and understand the nature of its language, we may avoid much trouble and serious difficulty. (21 April 1878, JD, 19:341.)

We made a covenant to follow the Spirit. When we received this gospel, we covenanted before God that we would be led, that we would be governed, and would follow the suggestions of the Holy Spirit, that we would follow the suggestions of the principle that gives life, that gives knowledge, that gives understanding of the things of God, that communicates the mind of God; and that we would labor for the accomplishment of the purposes of God in the salvation of the human family, adopting as a motto of life, "The kingdom of God, or nothing." (8 April 1880, CR, p. 79.)

The Spirit is our friend. The Spirit is in every man and every woman so that they need not walk in the darkness at all, and it is not always necessary for them to come to the President of the Church, or to the Twelve, or to the elders of Israel to get counsel; they have it within them. There is a friend that knows just exactly what to say to them. From the time we receive the gospel, go down into the waters of baptism and have hands laid upon us afterwards for the gift of the Holy Ghost, we have a friend, if we do not drive it from us by doing wrong. That friend is the Holy Spirit, the Holy Ghost, which partakes of the things of God and shows them unto us. This is a grand means that the Lord has provided for us, that we may know the light, and not be groveling continually in the dark. (9 April 1899, CR, p. 52.)

The Spirit was never needed more than now. We are entirely dependent upon the spirit of inspiration, and if there ever was a time, since Adam occupied the Garden of Eden, when the Spirit of God was more needed than at the present time, I am not aware of it. (6 May 1889, DW, 38:762.)

The Spirit will lead us to do right. What can we wish for more than is comprehended in our religion? If we will stand firm upon the rock, and will follow the Spirit that has been placed in our bosoms, we shall act right in the way of our duties—we shall act right to those who are placed over us—we shall act right, whether in the light or in the dark. (11 October 1857, JD, 5:314.)

We must depend on the Spirit. We ought to understand—and I presume that we do generally—that the work which we have come into this life to perform cannot be done to the glory of God or to the satisfaction of ourselves merely by our own natural intelligence. We are dependent upon the Spirit of the Lord to aid us and to manifest to us from time to time what is necessary for us to accomplish under the peculiar circumstances that may surround us. It is the privilege of Latter-day Saints, when they get into difficulties, to have supernatural power of God, and in faith, day by day, to secure from the circumstances which may surround us that which will be beneficial and advance us in the principles of holiness and sanctification, that we may as far as possible be like our Father. (6 October 1898, CR, p. 2.)

Listening to the Spirit is not enough. Now, if we really desire to draw near to God; if we wish to place ourselves in accord with the good spirits of the eternal worlds; if we wish to establish within ourselves that faith which we read about and by which ancient Saints performed such wonderful works, we must, after we obtain the Holy Spirit, hearken to its whisperings and conform to its suggestions, and by no act of our lives drive it from us. (6 May 1882, JD, 23:192.)

We can do nothing without the Spirit. We have not the power to do anything without the assistance of the Spirit of the Lord. (9 April 1857, JD, 5:65.)

The impossible may be accomplished with the Spirit. There are many important things required at our hands, and many things which we can do, when assisted by the Spirit of the Lord, which may at times seem almost impossible to accomplish. (6 April 1898, CR, p. 12.)

The Spirit enables us to face every difficulty. "The spirit is given to every man to profit withal. To one is given faith." Not a common ordinary faith, which some people pretend to at the present day; but a faith which enables its possessors to be sawn asunder, to be cast into dens of lions, fiery furnaces, and to undergo tortures of every description. This was the kind of faith that the Holy Ghost conferred upon those who possessed it, enabling its possessor to stand in the midst of every difficulty, defy every opposition and lay down his life, if necessary, for the cause that he had espoused. There was an almighty inspiring power in this faith, given by the Lord through the Holy Ghost, which no other principle could communicate. (14 January 1872, JD, 14:303.)

We should sacrifice to obtain the Spirit. As Saints of God, elders of Israel, we should be willing to devote time and labor, making every necessary sacrifice in order to obtain the proper spiritual qualifications to be highly useful in our several callings. And may the Lord inspire every heart with the importance of these matters that we may seek diligently and energetically for the gifts and powers promised in the gospel we have obeyed. (6 May 1882, JD, 23:195.)

The ancient Israelites were without the Spirit. [Elder Snow read Exodus 14:10-15.] It appears that the children of Israel at the time referred to in the passage I have read, were not very well acquainted with the Lord, or with His ability to carry out His purposes. They, however, had not the opportunities of becoming acquainted with Him, as have the Latter-day Saints. They had seen some of the works of the Lord wrought in the presence of the Egyptians as well as in their own presence; but their hearts had not been touched, neither had their understandings been enlightened by the intelligence of the Holy Spirit, as has been the case with the Latter-day Saints; and therefore, when they were brought to face the Red Sea, which, to all human appearance, was impassable, and with the armies of the Egyptians pressing close upon them, their hearts failed them. (7 April 1882, JD, 23:150.)

The Spirit removes part of the veil. I see before me this afternoon thousands of people who have received the gospel of Christ from among the various nations of the earth. They have made sacrifices which have astonished the world at large. Leaving all that was near and dear to them they have come and settled in these mountain vales, exposing themselves to danger both upon sea and land, and journeyed to a place of which they knew comparatively little. What inspired them to do this? The Spirit of God opened their understanding; it removed part of the veil which hung between them and the knowledge of God, and they became convinced by His power and intelligence of a supernatural nature that there was something which could not be reached through any other source of life, through any other system or order of things than the gospel which had been proclaimed to them. (5 October 1889, JH, p. 5.)

We may receive revelation every day. There is a way by which persons can keep their consciences clear before God and man, and that is to preserve within them the Spirit of God, which is the spirit of revelation to every man and woman. It will reveal to them, even in the simplest of matters, what they shall do, by making suggestions to them. We should try to learn the nature of this spirit, that we may understand its suggestions, and then we will always be able to do right. This is the grand privilege of every Latter-day Saint. We know that it is our right to have the manifestations of the Spirit every day of our lives. (9 April 1899, CR, p. 52.)

The greatest principles come through the Spirit. Of course we learn a great many things through reflection and by the exercise of the intelligence which we have acquired through the cultivation of the principles of truth; but those things which are of the greatest importance to the Latter-day Saints are derived through the revelations of the Holy Spirit. Many principles of vast importance, principles that will assist greatly through all the scenes of life, may be developed through the revelations of the Holy Spirit on occasions of this kind when we come together to hear the word of the Lord through His servants. (5 October 1882, JD, 23:288.)

What we gain from general conference depends on our closeness to the Spirit. I wish to remind the Latter-day Saints that the advantages we receive today or tomorrow, while gathered here, will be according to the spirit that we exercise individually. The elders may address you here, and yet no particular advantage is secured unless you have the Spirit and exercise the faith that it is our privilege to exercise, that we may be blessed to understand such things as may be spoken. (6 October 1900, CR, p. 23.)

We need the Spirit in order to speak. You know that it is impossible for us to address a congregation of Latter-day Saints in a manner to satisfy ourselves, unless we have the promptings of the Spirit of the Almighty. (6 May 1889, DW, 38:762.)

Pray that speakers will be guided by the Spirit. One of the greatest prayers that a man can offer, so far as I understand prayers and their consistency, is that when an elder of Israel stands before the people, he may communicate and tell some thoughts to do the people good, and build them up in the principles of truth and salvation. Prayers of this kind are as agreeable in the ears of the Lord as any prayers that an elder of Israel can possibly offer, for when an elder stands before the people he should do so realizing that he stands before them for the purpose of communicating knowledge, that they may receive truth in their souls and be built up in righteousness by receiving further light, progressing in their education in the principles of holiness.

This cannot be done, except by a labor of mind, by an energy of faith, and by seeking with all one's heart the Spirit of the Lord our God. (18 January 1857, JD, 4:182.)

The Spirit, not miracles, brings faith. The nature and the character of those teachings that come from the priesthood are such that we comprehend them; the Spirit manifests them unto us as they are. By it we learn our duties to God and man. We are taught by it to shun the evil and cleave unto that which is good. We understand this, if we are in the path of duty. It is not miracles that produce within us that living faith of which President Young so frequently speaks; but we learn the nature and character of our religion. (7 April 1861, JD, 9:21-22.)

The Spirit teaches us our duty. We may increase in knowledge and power, and in our ability to build up the kingdom of God upon the earth, and that, too, by our diligence, our humility, and faithfulness to the covenants we have made. We do not require miracles to enable us to perform the duties of today. We know, from defending the teachings of the servants of God, that we are right—that the Spirit from on high accompanies us. We know that we are right as well as the Lord does. How do we know this? Because Deity is within us, and that Spirit of Deity that is within us teaches us that we are the sons of God; it teaches the sisters that they are the daughters of God, and by it we are all taught that we are the children of our Father in Heaven. Therefore we know if we are in the line of our duty. (7 April 1861, JD, 9:22-23.)

We should seek education of the Spirit. I feel to say a word or two in reference to education. There are very few people who have arrived at the age of fifty and upwards who feel like studying mathematics; they do not feel like attending school and applying their minds to the acquisition of the sciences, but there is a kind of education worthy the best attention of all, and in which all ought to engage—that is the education of the Spirit. As we advance in life we one and all ought to be less passionate, more spiritually minded. (9 October 1867, JD, 12:147.)

All knowledge is prompted of the Spirit. Every unfoldment of the nineteenth century in science, in art, in mechanism, in music, in literature, in poetic fancy, in philosophical thought, was prompted by His Spirit which before long will be poured out upon all flesh that will receive it. He is the Father of us all and He desires to save and exalt us all. (1 January 1901, MFP, 3:335.)

The Spirit brings happiness. All this trouble and vexation of mind is but a matter of the present; and if we keep the light of the Spirit within us, we can so walk in the gospel that we can measurably enjoy happiness in this world; and while we are traveling onward, striving for peace and happiness that lie in our path, in the distance, we shall have a peace of mind that none can enjoy but those who are filled with the Holy Spirit. (11 October 1857, JD, 5:313.)

CHAPTER 16

Sacrifice, Suffering, and Trials

The Saints must be willing to sacrifice all. We have found the treasure in the field, we have found the pearl of great price, and now we have got to give all that we have for it, at one time or another. The Lord has said that He will prove us even unto death, to see whether we will stand by the covenants we have made with Him. Some Latter-day Saints have things in their possession which are so valuable to them that they would prefer death to the loss of those things. We have to deal with facts, not a mere ideal. In one sense, it is a hard thing for us to sell all that we have that we may secure these glories that have been opened to our view; but it will pay us in the end. (18 May 1899, MS, 61:530-31.)

Men who are not willing to sacrifice are worth little. The Lord very possibly may cause a heavy pressure to bear upon us, such as will require great sacrifice at the hands of His people. The question with us is, will we make that sacrifice? This work is the work of the Almighty, and the blessings we look for which have been promised, will come after we have proven ourselves and passed through the ordeal. I have no special word to this people that there is, or that there is not, before them a fiery ordeal through which they will be called to pass; the question with me is, am I prepared to receive and put to a right and proper use any blessing the Lord has in store for me in common with His people; or on the other hand, am I prepared to make any sacrifice that He may require at my hands? I would not give the ashes of a rye straw for any religion that was not worth living for and that was not worth dying for; and I would not give much for the man that was not willing to sacrifice his all for the sake of his religion. (7 April 1882, JD, 23:155.)

We should be a self-sacrificing people. Now, the Lord having manifested to the Latter-day Saints this principle of immortality and continuance of advancement, in the past they have shown most clearly and fully that they have been willing to sacrifice whatever they might possess and to go through the most undesirable experiences rather than turn aside from the path of exaltation and glory and give up the hopes God had inspired within them. Having had these grand and glorious prospects, which no language can express, unfolded to our view, we ought to be the best, the most virtuous and the most self-sacrificing people on the face of the globe. (5 April 1901, CR, p. 2.)

Be willing to sacrifice as Esther was. It may become necessary in the future—and this is the point I wish to make—for some of the Saints to act the part of Esther, the queen, and be willing to sacrifice anything and everything that is required at their hands for the purpose of working out the deliverance of the Latter-day Saints. (5 October 1882, JD, 23:290.)

The greatest sacrifices require the Spirit. No mortal man could have done what Abraham did—taking up on Mount Moriah his only son as a sacrifice—except he were inspired and had a divinity within him to receive that inspiration. We read of these extraordinary manifestations in the lives of the prophets. We find men at the present day that never could have done what they have done, never could have made the sacrifices they have, unless there had been a receiving and comprehending of the language of divinity—the Spirit. (10 April 1898, CR, p. 64.)

Some have sacrificed all for the kingdom of God. It has proved very truly with the Latter-day Saints what Jesus said on a certain occasion, when He compared the kingdom of God to a man seeking pearls. Having found one of very great value, he went and sold all that he possessed that he might secure that pearl. Then again He compared it unto a man that found a treasure in a field, which, having found, he went and sold everything that he possessed in order that he might come in possession of that treasure. That has been the case with the Latter-day Saints. We have been called to suffer and to sacrifice that which was more dear to ourselves than our lives, and some have been called to sacrifice their mortal existence, having been placed in circumstances that they could not avoid suffering the loss of their lives. We are called upon daily to make sacrifices. (10 April 1898, CR, p. 62.)

Sacrifice brings the treasures of eternity. We are His Saints, His Sons, and His daughters, and all things are open to us; the treasures of time and of eternity are ours—everything is ours, if we will serve our God in faithfulness, even to the sacrifice of all we possess. There lies the preparation for happiness hereafter. (11 October 1857, JD, 5:317.)

Suffering leads toward exaltation. I suppose I am talking to some who have had worry and trouble and heart burnings and persecution, and have at times been caused to think that they never expected to endure quite so much. But for everything you have suffered, for everything that has occurred to you which you thought an evil at that time, you will receive fourfold, and that suffering will have had a tendency to make you better and stronger and to feel that you have been blessed. When you look back over your experiences you will then see that you have advanced far ahead and have gone up several rounds of the ladder toward exaltation and glory. (15 June 1901, DN, p. 1.)

Sanctification requires suffering. Take it individually or take it collectively, we have suffered and we shall have to suffer again;

and why? Because the Lord requires it at our hands for our sanctification. (7 October 1857, JD, 5:323.)

Our suffering is for the same reason as Christ's. It has not been with the Latter-day Saints the most delightful thing that could be imagined to suffer as they have suffered—and what for? For the same as Jesus suffered, to a certain extent—for the salvation of the world. And although in this life very many of them may not receive that which we offer to them, the day will come, through the progress of things in eternity, when they will receive it, and they will be thankful that we came into the world and suffered in their interests as we have. (5 April 1901, CR, p. 3.)

Do not compromise to avoid suffering. Some of our brethren have queried whether hereafter they could feel themselves worthy of full fellowship with prophets and Saints of old, who endured trials and persecutions; and with Saints of our own times who suffered in Kirtland, in Missouri, and Illinois. The brethren referred to have expressed regrets that they had not been associated in those scenes of suffering. If any of these are present, I will say, for the consolation of such, you have to wait but a short time and you will have similar opportunities, to your heart's content. You and I cannot be made perfect except through suffering; Jesus could not. In His prayer and agony in the Garden of Gethsemane, He foreshadowed the purifying process necessary in the lives of those whose ambition prompts them to secure the glory of a celestial kingdom. None should try to escape by resorting to any compromising measures. "All who journey soon or late, Must come within the garden gate, And kneel alone in darkness there, And battle hard, yet not despair." (10 January 1886, JD, 26:367.)

We should be willing to suffer for each other. Now when a man is not willing to sacrifice for the benefit of his brethren, and when he knows that he trespasses upon the feelings of his brethren, and yet he has not that love which will enable him to make satisfaction, that man is not right before the Lord, and where is the love of that individual for his brother?

When one brother is not willing to suffer for his brother, how is it in his power to manifest that he has love for his brother? I tell you it is in our folly and weakness that we will not bear with our brethren, but if they trespass upon our rights we immediately retaliate, and if they tread upon our toes we immediately jump upon theirs, the same as the people do in the Gentile world, where it is thought necessary to act in a state of independence, and to defend oneself against aggressors.

It is all nonsense for us any longer to act upon this principle, for there is a day coming that we will have to suffer for each other, and even be willing to lay down our lives for each other, as Jesus did for the Twelve Apostles in His day, and as they did for the cause which He established. When I see a brother that has been trespassed against, and then he turns round and jumps upon the offender, then I say, how far is that brother from the path of duty, and I say to him you must learn to govern yourself, or you never will be saved in the kingdom of God. (4 January 1857, JD, 4:158.)

Mortality is a school of suffering and trials. We are here that we may be educated in a school of suffering and of fiery trials, which school was necessary for Jesus, our Elder Brother, who, the scriptures tell us, "was made perfect through suffering." It is necessary that we suffer in all things, that we may be qualified and worthy to rule, and govern all things, even as our Father in Heaven and His eldest son, Jesus. (1 December 1851, MS, 13:363.)

Salvation is impossible without trials. Peter, James, and John came down from heaven and ordained men to preach the gospel; we have that priesthood, and we must expect to suffer more or less as Jesus suffered. It is impossible for us to work out our salvation and accomplish the purposes of God without trials or without sacrifices. (18 April 1887, MS, 49:245.)

God is feeling after us. God is now feeling after us, and will disclose our secret thoughts. It would be well to purify and prepare ourselves, and in the language of the Psalmist, call upon God, saying, "Search me, O God, and know my heart: try me, and know my thoughts: and see if there be any wicked way in me, and lead me in the way everlasting."

If we succeed in passing through the approaching fiery ordeals with our fidelity and integrity unimpeached, we may expect at the close of our trials, a great and mighty outpouring of the Spirit and power of God—a great endowment upon all who shall have remained true to their covenants. (10 January 1886, JD, 26:366.)

Trials prove our dependability. The trials and temptations have been very great to many of our people, and more or less, perhaps, to all of us. The Lord seems to require some proof on our part, something to show that He can depend upon us when He wants us to accomplish certain things in His interest. The reason is that the condition in which we will be placed in the future, as time passes along, as eternity approaches, and as we move forward in eternity and along the line of our existence, we shall be placed in certain conditions that require very great sacrifice in the interests of humanity, in the interests of the Spirit of God, in the interest of His children and our own children, in generations to come, in eternity. Jesus Christ the Son of God was once placed in a condition that it required the highest effort in order to accomplish what was necessary for the salvation of millions of the children of God. It required the highest effort and determination that had to be exercised before the Son of God could pass through the ordeal, the sacrifice that was necessary. (5 October 1900, CR, p. 2.)

There are tens of thousands of Latter-day Saints that can testify to the truth of this work. They know it for themselves; but I fear there are too many that have not secured that assurance that is absolutely necessary, because every man and every woman will be tried to see how far he or she has an understanding in regard to these principles. (1 June 1895, DW, 50:738.)

Severe trials bring perfect faith. "But you have need of patience, that after you have done the will of God, you may receive the promise," a caution which should not be forgotten. Many of you may have severe trials, that your faith may become more perfect, your confidence be increased, and your knowledge of the powers of heaven be augmented; and this before your redemption takes place. If a stormy cloud sweep over the horizon of your course in this land, as in America—if the cup of bitter suffering be offered and you be compelled to partake—if Satan is let loose among you, with all his seductive powers of deceiving and cunning craftiness—if the strong relentless arm of persecution is against you, then, in that hour lift up your heads and rejoice that you are accounted worthy to suffer with Jesus, the Saints, and holy prophets, and know that the period of your redemption approaches. (1 December 1851, MS, 13:364; BLS, pp. 196-97.)

Trials are blessings in disguise. They the Saints may be afflicted and pass through numerous trials of a severe character, but these will prove blessings in disguise and bring them out brighter and better than they were before. The people of God are precious in His sight; His love for them will always endure, and in His might and strength and affection, they will triumph and be brought off more than conquerer. They are His children, made in His image and destined through obedience to His laws to become like unto Him. (8 October 1898, DW, 57:514.)

The Latter-day Saints, by being wise and prudent, can make this life a tolerably happy one. We need not live in misery; we need not feel that we are sacrificing all the time, but that what we call sacrifices prove a blessing to us, which we would not receive were it not for this experience. Everything that transpires affecting us individually may be made a blessing, and will be a blessing to us if we act wisely and prudently. (6 October 1899, CR, p. 2.)

Do not shrink from trials. Brethren and sisters, you and I have received light and intelligence, and we know whereof we speak; we know that these principles that we have espoused are true. We know that if we are faithful, and if we do not shrink from under the various trials and afflictions that may arise, that our salvation is secure. We know there is a place in yonder worlds for every man and woman who prove faithful to their covenants. (18 April 1887, MS, 49:243.)

Without trials there is no deliverance. Where the Lord plants us, there we are to stand: when He requires us to exert ourselves for the support of these holy principles, that we are to do; that is all we need to trouble ourselves about; the rest our Heavenly Father will take care of. But it need not surprise us that difficulties and storms arise—that we see hurricanes playing about us—that we see war-clouds gather thick and fast about us; this need not be surprising. Where there is no trial there can be no deliverance; where there is no temptation, the power of God cannot be made manifest to any great extent. (7 October 1857, JD, 5:323.)

Only by the Spirit can we overcome trials. We are bound to rise and to advance in power and in influence in the midst of the world. There may, as has been suggested by one of the speakers, be opposition to meet of a nature that we have never met before; such things have come in the past, and will come in the future; but I will assure you that if we will do our duty with a determination that we will be prepared for everything; we will go through successfully any future difficulties that may arise no matter how serious they may be. We have done wonders; we have passed through difficulties and made sacrifices that are marvelous, when we consider their nature. And we have done, and will do in the future, that which we never could have done unless we had educated ourselves by the Spirit and power of God. We are a mighty people, and growing mightier as trials and difficulties arise. (9 October 1898, CR, p. 55.)

The Lord will help us overcome trials. From the time of our receiving the gospel to the present, the Lord has from time to time given us trials and afflictions if we may so call them; and sometimes these trials have been of that nature that we have found it very difficult to receive them without murmur and complaint. Yet at such times the Lord blessed us and gave us sufficient of His Spirit to enable us to overcome the temptations and endure the trials. In going through these trials and troubles we are doing no more than did the captain of our salvation. We are told by the Apostle Paul that He was made perfect through sufferings. And even He, the Son of God, at times found it very difficult. For example, in the Garden of Gethsemane, when the time approached that He was to pass through the severest affliction that any mortal ever did pass through, He undoubtedly had seen persons nailed to the cross, because that method of execution was common at that time, and He understood the torture that such persons experienced for hours. He went by Himself in the garden and prayed to His Father, if it were possible, that that cup might pass from Him; and His feelings were such that He sweat great drops of blood, and in His agony there was an angel sent to give Him comfort and strength. Even the Son of God required miraculous help under those extraordinary circumstances. So we have needed it at times, and so we may in the future. (4 November 1893, DW, 47:609.)

The Lord knows how to help us overcome difficulties. We have found undoubtedly in our experience that it requires something of a desirable nature to incite us to action. If a person had a strong idea that there was a very precious mine undiscovered in one of these mountains east he would travel along the road to secure its discovery, and would be willing to make many sacrifices and perform much labor and toil in order to get at that mine, and he would endure the scorn that he might hear daily while endeavoring to reach this. This is natural. The Lord knew our natures and dispositions, and He knew exactly what to place before us in order to stimulate us to that course of action which will enable us to overcome the various difficulties that arise in our path of progress. (3 November 1894, DW, 49:609.)

Many difficulties arise through indifference. God bless you, my brethren and sisters. Do not be discouraged. The path may be rough, but much of its roughness arises from our own indifference and carelessness. It would be much smoother if we would diligently observe the commandments of God and keep the Spirit of the Lord continually in our hearts. Yet, after all, there are sacrifices to make, but in making these sacrifices there is a possibility of having enjoyment in the anticipation of what will be the final result. (3 November 1894, DW, 49:610.)

Trials have caused many to fall. Latter-day Saints possessing the highest abilities have fallen. I could refer to many in the days of Kirtland, and right along till the present time, where persons have been blessed with great abilities, and have accomplished a great deal for the cause of God; but when trials and obstacles arose in their path, they failed to perform their duties, and turned away and became apostates to the Church, and all their past labors amounted to nothing. (18 April 1887, MS, 49:244.)

The gates of hell shall not prevail against us. Now, Latter-day Saints, how is it with us? We have received the gospel. We have received the kingdom of God, established on the earth. We have had trouble; we have been persecuted. We were driven from Ohio; we were driven from Missouri; we were driven from Nauvoo; and once we were driven for a time from this beautiful city [Salt Lake City]. Many have lost thousands of dollars; lost their homes and all they had, and some of the brethren have seen their wives and children lay down their lives because of the hardships they had to experience during these changes, these persecutions, these revolutions, and these drivings. The people have looked with astonishment at the willingness of the Latter-day Saints to suffer these things. Why do we do this? Why do we adhere to these principles that have caused us at times so much grief and sacrifice? What is it that enables us to endure these persecutions and still rejoice? It is because we have had revelations from the Almighty; because He has spoken to us in our souls and has given to us the Holy Ghost, which is a principle of revelation wherever it exists and is promised to every man, as in the days of the former Apostles, who will believe, repent of his sins and be immersed in water for the remission of them by those who have the authority from the Lord to administer this ordinance. Jesus, when He was among the children of men, said that He would build His church upon this principle of revelation and the gates of hell should not prevail against it. (6 April 1900, CR, pp. 2-3.)

Job's victory over his trials is a consolation to the Lord's people. I wonder if there are a few here within the sound of my voice that have feelings of this kind, like old Job had, for instance. A poor man who wondered why his children were taken from him; why his herds were destroyed and why his houses, his dwelling, went up in flames, and why he was left without anything. He formerly was a very wealthy man, then was left without anything. Well, his friends came about him. They were supposed to be friends. They were friends formerly. They came about him and wanted to show him that these evils came upon him because he had failed to do his duty in the past; because he had committed some sin. That was the kind of ideas that they communicated to him. But there was nothing of the kind. It was not so. They were vastly mistaken. The Lord had a certain position in which He sought to place Job in the future at some future time when years and years had rolled away perhaps, and He wanted to try him. He wanted to educate him so that he would not complain, no matter how illy he thought himself treated by the Lord. That was a glorious trial of Job's. It has come down in history, his experiences and his trials; and it has been a wonderful consolation to the people of the Lord to read the history of his experiences and his trials and how well he passed through them. (5 October 1900, CR, p. 4.)

We should seek to be like Job. The religion that we have received, the principles of exaltation and glory that you and I have received, bring upon us persecution, or else they are not those principles which we thought they were. They bring upon us trouble upon the right hand and upon the left, but we should seek to be calm and cool as Job learned to be calm and cool under circumstances of the most unhappy character. We should learn to do this and there are things that are provided for us by which we can learn this. Think now of how much worse you and I might be, and then think of what superior blessings we actually possess. (5 October 1900, CR, p. 4.)

The Saints can glorify God by rising above their trials. The world, which knows not the purposes of God, may think that "Mormonism" is now about to be destroyed, that the voice of the Latter-day Saints and the priesthood will never be heard again throughout the world; but when these dark clouds thicken about us, and the Saints are put to the test, it is then that God is more glorified, in the fact that we are ready to show our willingness to pass through the fiery ordeal. We make no complaint, but feel thankful that we are able to show how precious is to us the religion which we have espoused. Let us go on rejoicing. (5 October 1889, JH, p. 5.)

Do not cease to persevere. I have noticed that many young ladies, and young men, too, start in to learn music, but get discouraged, and, failing to persevere, they do not succeed in accomplishing that which they undertook. You may notice the same thing among the Latter-day Saints. Persons get baptized, and they feel to rejoice in the gospel and that which is unfolded to them. They prosper well for a time, but after awhile they cease to persevere; they become soured, perhaps, at some things they experience in their acquaintance with their brethren who, perchance, are not wise, and they turn their backs upon the principles in which they took so much delight in the beginning, and go into darkness. (3 April 1897, DW, 54:482.)

Those who endure to the end will receive all things. It is a grand position that we occupy. Our future is glorious. We could not desire more for our happiness than has been prepared for us. Those who endure unto the end shall sit upon thrones, as Jesus hath overcome and sat down upon His Father's throne. All things shall be given unto such men and women, so we are told in the revelations we have received. In view of these prospects, what should we not be willing to sacrifice when duty requires? (9 October 1898, CR, pp. 55-56.)

CHAPTER 17

The Ways of the World

Forget Worldly Matters. We should endeavor as far as possible to forget all worldly matters which grieve and vex us, and fix our minds upon the Lord, having a sufficiency of His Holy Spirit that we may be enabled to receive such knowledge and suggestions as will help us in our onward path.

I believe there never was a time since the organization of this Church and kingdom of God upon the earth when it was more necessary than now for us to obtain spiritual aid and blessings, in order that we may be prepared for the great event which seems now to be rapidly approaching. (5 October 1889, JH, p. 4.)

Some who were faithful succumb to love of the world. There are men among us upon whom the Spirit of the Almighty once rested mightily, whose intentions were once as good and pure as those of angels, and who made covenants with God that they would serve Him and keep His commandments under every and all circumstances; and many of such were ready and willing to leave their wives and children to go or come as the case might be in the interest of the cause they had espoused. But how is it now with some of those elders? They do not feel so today. Their affections are set upon the things of this world which the Lord has enabled them to acquire, that they wait now until they are called, and in many instances when called, they obey more out of a desire to retain their standing and position than a real heart-felt love of the labor to which they may have been called.

This is the condition of all men, no matter how well they start out, who allow their thoughts and affections to run after the world and its ways, and it is a plain and indisputable proof that when this is the case with men they love the world more than they love the Lord and His work upon the earth. (6 May 1882, JD, 23:194.)

Too often we stoop to the level of the world. One of the chief difficulties that many suffer from is that we are too apt to forget the great object of life, the motive of our Heavenly Father in sending us here to put on mortality, as well as the holy calling with which we have been called; and hence, instead of rising above the little transitory things of time, we too often allow ourselves to come down to the level of the world without availing ourselves of the divine help which God has instituted, which alone can enable us to overcome them. We are no better than the rest of the world if we do not cultivate the feeling to be perfect, even as our Father in Heaven is perfect. (7 April 1879, JD, 20:191.)

The cares of this life lead to weakness. It is the case with many in this community that instead of preparing themselves for positions in the eternal world, they have been satisfied with the cares of this life, and attending to those things which have been for the comfort of themselves and their wives and children; they have been satisfied in exercising themselves in this small way of ambition. They have forgotten the salvation of their forefathers, and that on them lay the responsibility of laying a holy and pure foundation upon which their posterity may build and obtain life and salvation, and upon which the generations to come might return back to their pristine purity. Instead of being sanctified this day as the people might have been had they sought it diligently, they are weak in their intellects, weak in their faith, weak in their power in reference to the things of God, and many of them this day, setting aside their being saviors of men, are incapable of administering salvation to their individual wives and children. This, brethren, whatever you may think about it, is a solemn consideration. (4 January 1857, JD, 4:155.)

We should not be satisfied with the perishable things of time. We have received a gospel that is marvelous in its operations: through obedience to its requirements we may receive the choicest blessings that have ever been promised to or bestowed upon mankind in any age of the world. But, like the child with the toy or the plaything, we too often satisfy ourselves with the perishable things of time, forgetting the opportunities we have of developing within us the great, the eternal principles of life and truth. (6 May 1882, JD, 23:193.)

Our actions should not be motivated by worldly approval. Some are induced to do certain things in order to receive the approbation of their friends, and if their acts fail to draw forth favorable comments or to be recognized, they feel as though their labor had been lost and what good they may have done was a total failure. (6 May 1882, JD, 23:192.)

We must overcome the world. The god of the world is the gold and the silver. The world worships this god. It is all-powerful to them, though they might not be willing to acknowledge it. Now it is designed, in the providence of God, that the Latter-day Saints should show whether they have so far advanced in the knowledge, in the wisdom and in the power of God that they cannot be overcome by the god of the world. We must come to that point. We have also got to reach another standard, a higher plane; we have got to love God more than we love the world, more than we love gold or silver, and love our neighbor as ourselves. (6 May 1889, DW, 38:763.)

Worldliness impedes spiritual progress. There is no doubt, speaking of the people as a whole, that we are greatly improving in the sight of God. But although this is undoubtedly the case, I am convinced there are persons among us endowed with spiritual gifts and susceptible of cultivation that could be exercised, if they chose, to a far greater extent than they are, and who could move much faster in the ways of holiness and get much nearer to the Lord. But the spirit which attends the things of this world is operating upon them to that extent that they do not increase those spiritual powers and blessings; they do not place themselves in that close relationship to the Lord that it is their privilege. (6 May 1882, JD, 23:194.)

Beware of the ways of the world. Ye toiling millions who, in the sweat of your faces earn your daily bread, look up and greet the power from above which shall lift you from bondage! The day of your redemption draweth nigh. Cease to waste your wages in that which helps to keep you in want. Regard not wealth as your enemy and your employers as your oppressors. Seek for the union of capital and labor. Be provident when in prosperity. Do not become a prey to designing men who seek to stir up strife for their own selfish ends. Strive for your rights by lawful means, and desist from violence and destruction. Anarchism and lawlessness are your deadly foes. (1 January 1901, MFP, 3:334.)

Worldliness harms our relationship with God. If, after the expiration of fifty years, we as a community do not stand in that high relationship to God that we could wish, the fault is not in the Lord, it is not for the lack of information placed before us, but that lack is in ourselves; it arises from our ignorance or neglect, or from a desire, peradventure, to serve the spirit of the world instead of the Spirit of God. (8 April 1880, CR, p. 80.)

Do not envy your neighbor. If we are poor, and have not as much as our neighbor possesses, do not envy him, and do not worry about it. As I said in the beginning of my remarks, there is an eternity before us, and we shall always be ourselves, and nobody else, and what we do not gain today we will gain tomorrow, or some other time. (5 April 1901, CR, p. 3.)

CHAPTER 18

The Family: An Eternal Unit

We are to multiply and replenish the earth. One of the first commandments that God gave when He introduced the human family upon this little globe upon which we dwell was that they should multiply and replenish the earth. That was a matter of the highest importance, or God would never have given that commandment. It was of the utmost importance that the earth should be peopled with the sons and daughters of God. (1 June 1895, DW, 50:737.)

We should work to establish union in the family. Should there not be union in the family? Should there not be union with the husband, who is the high priest in his family and expects to be with them in the next life? Should there not be a perfect union with him and his wife, and his sons, his daughters, his sons-in-law, and his daughters-in-law? Most assuredly there should. And why should any man be satisfied, why should any husband and father of a family rest satisfied until he effects a perfect union, that is, just as far as a perfect union can be accomplished? And in this matter the father should make himself just as perfect as a man can in this life be made perfect before his family. And the wife should make herself just as perfect as a woman can possibly do in this life. And then they are prepared to make their children just as perfect as they are willing and are capable of being made perfect. And the father and the mother should be very careful. The wife should never in the presence of her children speak disrespectfully of her husband. If she thinks her husband has done wrong (he might have done), she should never speak of it in the presence of her children. She should take him out of the presence of her children and there tell him of his faults, in a pleasant way, but never in the presence of the children speak disrespectfully of the father. And the father the same. He has no right to speak disrespectfully of his wife in the presence of her children. And I pray God to give the husband and wife the spirit and the understanding to correct themselves in such matters. I know that a great many of the difficulties that now appear, and the disrespect that we find in reference to the priesthood among young people arises from this fact, that there have been difficulties in the home circle, and there has been disrespect expressed in their presence, of the father by the mother, or of the mother by the father. Now, I know these things are so. (5 October 1897, CR, pp. 32-33.)

Family unity must prevail in Zion. If you ever secure a union in any family in Zion, if you ever secure that heavenly union which is necessary to exist there, you have got to bind that family together in one, and there has got to be the Spirit of the Lord in the head of that family, and he should possess that light and that intelligence which, if carried out in the daily life and conduct of these individuals, will prove the salvation of that family, for he holds their salvation in his hands.

He goes to work, and associates his feelings and affections with theirs as far as lies in his power, and endeavors to secure all those things that are necessary for their comfort and welfare, and they on the other part have got to turn round and manifest the same feeling, the same kindness, and the same disposition, and to the utmost of their ability manifest feelings of gratitude for the blessings which they receive.

This is necessary, that there may be a oneness of feeling, or oneness of sentiment and a corresponding affection, that they, being one, may be bound together in this way. (1 March 1857, JD, 4:243.)

A father should counsel his children according to their needs. A father, in communicating counsel to his son, should in the first place prepare himself to communicate those proper counsels which will suit the condition of his son. It is his privilege to extend happiness to himself; it is his privilege to increase his own happiness, and in increasing his own happiness he should extend it throughout his family dominions. And when he is increasing his own happiness, his own glory, his own authority, he at the same time is increasing that of his children, provided that counsel which he reveals is all the time that which is best for his family. If good counsel was not established for the benefit of the individual that communicates it, also of those who receive it, it would be of no service. (18 January 1857, JD, 4:184.)

Our children follow our example. The husband has to learn to give proper counsel and direction; he has to learn how to manage his wife and his children, and it takes him some time to learn how to manage wisely and to bestow comfort upon each member of his family.

Our children, if we are diligent in cultivating in ourselves the pure principles of life and salvation, will grow up in the knowledge of these things, and be able with greater facility than ourselves to promote the orders of heaven and establish happiness and peace around them. (11 October 1857, JD, 5:315.)

Righteous fathers instruct their children. It is the business of the father to be qualified to teach and instruct his children, and to lay principles before them, so that by conforming to those instructions they can be the most happy that their natures are susceptible of in a state of childhood, while at the same time they learn the principles upon which they can gain the most happiness and enjoyment in a state of manhood. Those children are under obligations to follow their father's counsel precisely, so long as the counsel which the father gives is calculated for this express purpose. They are under obligations to follow that and carry it out in its design and in its object, and the moment they break off and separate themselves from the father they become like a branch that is separated from a tree; they no longer flourish nor bring forth fruit. The branch that is cut off from the tree ceases to have the life giving power, ceases to bring forth fruit. Let a person be cut off from this Church and he no longer remains a wise director and counselor for his children, but only so long as he has the privilege of receiving and having counsel in which is deposited that wisdom and knowledge and power that can give life to those that are around him. (18 January 1857, JD, 4:184-85.)

Fathers should teach the words of life to their families. It becomes the duties of fathers in Israel to wake up and become saviors of men, that they may walk before the Lord in that strength of faith, and that determined energy, that will insure them the inspiration of the Almighty to teach the words of life to their families, as well as to teach them when they are called into this stand. Then all our words will savor of life and salvation wherever we go, and wherever we are. (4 January 1857, JD, 4:158.)

A husband should value his wife. To the husbands I say: Many of you do not value your wives as you should—unless you are different from any audience of this size that I have ever had before me. Be kind to them. When they go out to meeting, you carry the baby at least half the time. When it needs rocking, and you have not much to do, rock it. Be kind when sometimes you have to make a little sacrifice to do so; feel kind anyway, no matter what the sacrifice. (20 July 1901, JH, p. 4.)

Husbands and fathers should be sensitive. The men ought to be more fatherly at home, possessing finer feelings in reference to their wives and children, neighbors and friends, more kindly and godlike. When I go into a family I do admire to see the head of that family administering to it as a man of God, kind and gentle, filled with the Holy Ghost and with the wisdom and understanding of heaven. Men and women can increase their spiritual knowledge. (9 October 1867, JD, 12:148.)

Fathers should seek the Spirit. The men who are sitting here this day ought to be, when in the presence of their families, filled with the Holy Ghost, to administer the word of life to them as it is administered in this stand from Sabbath to Sabbath. When they kneel down in the presence of their wives and children they ought to be inspired by the gift and power of the Holy Ghost, that the husband may be such a man as a good wife will honor, and that the gift and power of God may be upon them continually. They ought to be one in their families, that the Holy Ghost might descend upon them, and they ought to live so that the wife through prayer may become sanctified, that she may see the necessity of sanctifying herself in the presence of her husband, and in the presence of her children, that they may be one together, in order that the man and the wife may be pure element, suitable to occupy a place in the establishment and formation of the kingdom of God, that they may breathe a pure spirit and impart pure instruction to their children, and their children's children. (4 January 1857, JD, 4:155.)

Families progress by sustaining the father. If a father, for instance, had a large, extensive family, his object would be to do them good, to promote their interest and happiness, to put into their hands power, knowing that they could not accomplish much alone, and that they would have to take or obtain assistance from that family. The son that would take the deepest interest—that would devote himself the most faithfully to promote the designs of the father and head of that family, for the happiness and prosperity of the whole, would increase in power and influence faster than any other one; for the father would be disposed to put as much power and influence into his hands as it would be possible for him to receive, and as would be for the benefit of the family.

That would be the principle upon which all the members of that family would increase in knowledge, influence, and power above others. It would be by having the faculty, the feeling, and the disposition and desire to carry out the mind of the father, and that, too, for the benefit and exaltation of the whole family. (9 April 1857, JD, 5:63.)

Honor your father and mother. I would plead with you, my young brethren and sisters, to honor your fathers and your mothers, that your days may be long in the land which the Lord hath given to them and to you. Be obedient and loving to them; and after they have climbed to the summit of the hill of life, perhaps through many a hard-fought struggle, and begin to descend, try to do all in your power to make the road smooth and pleasant for them. By their devotion to you and to your welfare they have proved themselves worthy of your affection, and God expects you to be loyal to them. He has honored them in the past, and will yet honor them more abundantly; but their joy will not be fully complete if their children disregard their wishes and are untrue to them and to God. I therefore say to you, observe this commandment which God has given, to honor your fathers and your mothers. It is a commandment which carries with it the promise of longevity, and if you obey it there is every prospect for you to live to be as old as your parents, and even older.

Let your feet tread in the same path of advancement and progress as your parents; let your hearts beat in unison with theirs for the welfare of truth and righteousness, and by and by you will rejoice with them worlds without end. (2 July 1901, JH, p. 5.)

All will have an opportunity to marry. A lady came into our office the other day and asked to see me on a private matter. She informed me that she felt very badly, because her opportunities for getting a husband had not been favorable. She was about thirty years of age, and she wanted to know what her condition would be in the other life, if she did not succeed in getting a husband in this life. I suppose this question arises in the hearts of our young people, especially the marriageable sisters and the young widows; and some very foolish doctrine has been presented to some of the sisters in regard to this and other things of a kindred

nature. I desire to give a little explanation for the comfort and
consolation of parties in this condition. There is no Latter-day
Saint who dies after having lived a faithful life who will lose anything because of having failed to do certain things when opportunities were not furnished him or her. In other words, if a young
man or a young woman has no opportunity of getting married,
and they live faithful lives up to the time of their death, they will
have all the blessings, exaltation, and glory that any man or
woman will have who had this opportunity and improved it. That
is sure and positive. (18 May 1899, MS, 61:547.)

The Lord has promised an endless reign over our offspring.
An endless reign over our offspring, from all eternity to all eternity. Now, this is actually what the Lord has promised. It is not
anything that man has devised to entertain the imaginations of
people; but it is the word of God. (3 April 1897, DW, 54:481.)

Think of the promises that are made to you in the beautiful
and glorious ceremony that is used in the marriage covenant in
the temple. When two Latter-day Saints are united together in
marriage, promises are made to them concerning their offspring,
that reach from eternity to eternity. They are promised that they
shall have the power and the right to govern and control and
administer salvation and exaltation and glory to their offspring
worlds without end. And what offspring they do not have here,
undoubtedly there will be opportunities to have them hereafter.
What else could man wish? A man and a woman in the other life,
having celestial bodies, free from sickness and disease, glorified
and beautified beyond description, standing in the midst of their
posterity, governing and controlling them, administering life,
exaltation, and glory, worlds without end. (3 April 1897, DW,
54:481.)

Families should seek exaltation. Let families put themselves in
possession of all the good they can—be in a position to do right,
and be continually in the path to exaltation and glory. (11 October 1857, JD, 5:316.)

CHAPTER 19

Women and the Relief Society

Thank God for women. The thought has impressed itself upon me that the brethren of this Church, myself included, have been wonderfully favored of the Lord in having the companionship and assistance of such faithful, loyal wives and mothers as He has blessed us with. It is difficult to imagine what we should have done or what progress the work of the Lord would have made without them. When we have been absent on foreign missions, their missions at home have generally been no less arduous than ours abroad; and in the midst of trial and privation they have exhibited a patience, a fortitude, and a self-help that has been truly inspiring. Thank God for the women of this Church. (9 July 1901, JH, p. 5.)

Women stand by the priesthood. It has always been a source of pleasure to me to notice how faithfully you sisters of the Relief Society have stood by the servants of the Lord under all circumstances. You have ever been found at the side of the priesthood, ready to strengthen their hands and to do your part in helping to advance the interests of the kingdom of God; and as you have shared in these labors, so you will most certainly share in the triumph of the work and in the exaltation and glory which the Lord will give to His faithful children. (9 July 1901, JH, p. 5.)

Women are entitled to the Spirit. The Spirit of the gospel teaches every man who lives in the line of his duty that he is in the path of right, and so it does every woman. By it she knows she is walking in the path of truth and life. It is this Spirit which teaches the sisters as well as the brethren the right from the wrong; and she has a perfect right to know the truth of her religion—to have a knowledge for herself that the principles of her profession are divine. Is there anything wrong or mysterious in this? No. It is because she is a child of God, and therefore she is capacitated to know as he knows—to comprehend the principles of her religion, its divine origin, and its tendency onward and upward. (7 April 1861, JD, 9:23.)

Women should be patient with each other. It is so with you women. If any of you have more knowledge and influence than the others, more is required of you; you have the more to endure. (11 October 1857, JD, 5:316.)

If the Lord has made one woman more perfect than another, and given her more intelligence than her sisters, let her show more mercy and patience in overlooking their faults. By this means a wife will gain influence and favor with her husband, with her sisters, and with her Heavenly Father. She thus advances herself and puts herself in a position to enjoy all that is for the righteous. The whole is summed up in this—Do right. (11 October 1857, JD, 5:316.)

Sisters should be encouraged to honor the marriage covenant. I ask you, my sisters, in your visits to the homes of the Latter-day Saints, to carry this influence wherever you go. The Lord has clearly shown to you the nature of your relationship to Him and what is expected of you as wives and mothers. Teach these things to those whom you visit, especially to the young ladies. Encourage marriage among them, and impress upon them the sacredness of that relation and the obligation they are under to observe that great commandment which was given of God to our first parents, to multiply and replenish the earth. This is all the more necessary, in view of the present tendency in the world to disregard that law and to dishonor the marriage covenant. It is saddening to note the frequency of divorces in the land, and the growing inclination to look upon children as an encumbrance instead of as a precious heritage from the Lord. These evils should not gain a foothold among the people of God, and you, my sisters, as members of the Relief Society and as mothers in Israel, should exercise all your influence against them and in favor of pure motherhood and faithfulness to the marriage covenant. (9 July 1901, JH, p. 5.)

Sisters should indulge in recreation. Proper recreation and amusement are good things, and I am glad to see you sisters indulging in a little rest and recreation, for you who work so hard day after day in your homes and in the Relief Society certainly deserve all the enjoyment you can get. (9 July 1901, JH, p. 5.)

Wives, be faithful to your husbands. Wives, be faithful to your husbands. I know you have to put up with many unpleasant things, and your husbands have to put up with some things as well. Doubtless you are sometimes tried by your husbands, on account perhaps of the ignorance of your husbands, or perchance at times because of your own ignorance. I wonder if any of my sisters whom I am now addressing ever saw a time when they wished they had a better husband and perhaps entertained the idea of getting a divorce. I tell you how I used to do when I was president of the Box Elder Stake of Zion. Once in a while a woman would come to me with the information that she had been abused by her husband and she wanted a bill of divorce. "What has your husband done?" I would ask. Well, he had done such and such things. "Have you ever done wrong?" said I. Well, she thought perhaps she might have done wrong some-times. "Have you ever prayed that your husband might be a better man?" She did not know that she had prayed for him very hard, because at times he had been so abusive that she could scarcely exercise much faith in that direction. "Well," said I, "you go home and think about it; see if you have not been unwise sometimes and offended your husband; and go into a secret place and pray for him." I had at that time some very nice apples growing in an orchard which I had planted in an early day. One tree especially yielded some choice red apples, and I would pick six apples from that tree and give them to her, three for herself and three for her husband, and I would ask her to be sure and give him those three apples without saying that I gave them to her for that purpose. "Then," I said to her, "if things do not get better, in about two or three months come to me again and I will see what I can do for you." Well, the apples I gave and what I said to her accomplished the object. (20 July 1901, JH, p. 4.)

The Relief Society has a noble purpose. The mission of the Relief Society is to succor the distressed, to minister to the sick and feeble, to feed the poor, to clothe the naked, and to bless all the sons and daughters of God. No institution was ever founded with a nobler aim. Its basis is true charity, which is the pure love of Christ, and that spirit has been manifested in all the ministrations of the Society among the people. (9 July 1901, JH, p. 5.)

The Relief Society has a promising future. The future of the Society is full of promise. As the Church grows, its field of usefulness will be correspondingly enlarged, and it will be even more potent for good than it has been in the past. If all the sisters will rally to the support of the Society, it will accomplish a mighty work and be a continued blessing unto the Church. (9 July 1901, JH, p. 5.)

The Relief Society is a valuable adjunct to the priesthood. The Relief Society has been and is one of the most valuable adjuncts to the priesthood. It is in every deed a "help in government." And no wise bishop will fail to appreciate the labors of the Relief Society in his ward. What could a bishop do without a Relief Society? I would say to all the bishops in the Church, encourage the sisters of the Relief Society, and support them in their work of charity and benevolence, and they will prove a blessing to you and to the people. (9 July 1901, JH, p. 5.)

The Relief Society makes better wives and mothers. It might be thought by some that the labors connected with membership in the Relief Society would cause those sisters who belong to it to neglect their household duties. But this is not so. I will venture to say that the best wives and mothers and the most efficient house-keepers among us are members of the Relief Society, and I would advise the brethren to encourage their wives to join the society, where they can do so; for it would be a good thing to have the influence of this organization in every home. (9 July 1901, JH, p. 5.)

The Relief Society exemplifies pure religion. The Apostle James said that "pure religion and undefiled before God and the Father is this, to visit the fatherless and widows in their affliction, and to keep himself unspotted from the world." Accepting that as true, the members of the Relief Society have most surely exemplified in their lives pure and undefiled religion; for they have ministered to those in affliction, they have thrown their arms of love around the fatherless and the widows, and they have kept themselves unspotted from the world. I can testify that there are no purer and more God-fearing women in the world than are to be found within the ranks of the Relief Society. (9 July 1901, JH, p. 5.)

The Relief Society is performing a grand mission. I feel to say, God bless the officers and members of the Relief Society. You are performing a grand mission, and I would exhort you to not weary in well-doing. We are all aiming for celestial glory, and the grandeur of the prospects before us cannot be expressed in human language. If you will continue faithful to the work in which you are engaged, you will attain unto this glory, and rejoice evermore in the presence of God and the Lamb. This is worth striving for; it is worth sacrificing for, and blessed is the man or the woman who is faithful unto the obtaining of it. (9 July 1901, JH, p. 5.)

CHAPTER 20

Becoming One

The Saints must become one to accomplish the Lord's work. The Latter-day Saints are trying to do the work that Israel failed to do, and that the former Saints did not accomplish; and we can only do it by becoming one even as the Father and the Son are one, and this in order that the world may believe that we are sent of God. We have got to be perfect, and come to the measure of the stature of Christ Jesus, in order that the world may know that Jesus has sent and commissioned His Apostles, and restored the holy priesthood. If we have division in our midst; if we be divided either spiritually or temporally, we never can be the people that God designs us to become, nor can we ever become instruments in His hands of making the world believe that the holy priesthood has been restored, and that we have the everlasting gospel. (4 November 1882, JD, 23:341.)

We must effect a perfect union to attain exaltation. I believe there is a way by which perfect union can be effected if we will but understand things aright. Jesus urged upon His disciples the necessity of union—that the same should be promoted among them as existed between Himself and His Father. We must perfect ourselves before we can attain to the great exaltation and glory which have been promised unto the faithful. We should at all times be willing to make sacrifices for the gospel's sake, no matter how disagreeable the duty may sometimes be. (5 October 1889, JH, pp. 4-5.)

Each has a responsibility for unity. Had Moses, for instance, having done all that he did, had he delivered Israel from Egyptian bondage, and having done all that he could and all that mortal man could do for their redemption, having done all in his power, and been willing to lay down his life and to sacrifice everything that he had to accomplish that work, would he have secured the people to himself, and have brought about that union which was so necessary, without any exertion on their part? No, most assuredly it would not have been accomplished, for there had to be a return, an exertion on their part, in order to secure that union and that love, and to secure that fellowship between them and him, which it was necessary should exist, and so it is in reference to Jesus Christ; though He has sacrificed Himself and laid the plan for the redemption of the people, yet unless the people labor to obtain that union between Him and them, their salvation never will be accomplished. Thus we see that something has to be done by each party, in order to secure each other's friendship, and to bind us together as a community. (1 March 1857, JD, 4:240.)

We must become united to see God. We have just got to feel, brethren, that there are other people besides ourselves; we have got to look into the hearts and feelings of others, and become more godly than what we are now.

We should be bound together and act like David and Jonathan as the heart of one, and sooner let our arm be severed from our bodies than injure each other. What a mighty people we would be if we were in this condition, and we have got to go into it, however little feelings of friendship we may have in exercise at the present time. I can just tell you that the day will come when we must become united in this way if we ever see the presence of God. We shall have to learn to love our neighbors as we love ourselves. We must go into this, however far we are from it at the present time, yet no matter, we must learn these principles and establish them in our bosoms. (1 March 1857, JD, 4:245.)

We should seek the interests of others. Now you take a man that is continually looking after the interests of the people around him, and let him feel to bless anything and all things that belongs to his brethren, and he will in this way establish happiness in himself and around him. Let a man take the opposite course, and instead of blessing and laboring for the benefit of others, find fault and pull down, will he make the same improvement? Assuredly he will not. (1 March 1857, JD, 4:245-46.)

Always consider the feelings of others. The things of God have been revealed to this people, that they may go to work and obtain more faith and more confidence in God than any other people upon the face of the whole earth. We have to eat, drink, and clothe ourselves, as well as other people, but in gaining these things we should regard sacredly each other's rights. When two individuals are bound together, as they eventually must be if they ever stand in the presence of God, rather than to take a course to injure each other's feelings, when they are united as they should be and as they will be, they would sooner have a limb severed from their body, they would sooner suffer anything that could be executed upon them than to disturb or hurt each other's feelings. There would be the same love that existed between David and Jonathan. Before David would do anything to disturb the feelings of Jonathan, he would have suffered a hundredfold of trouble to come upon himself. I think we sometimes pass by those things which are of such great importance. I often think of the little anecdote that is recorded in the Bible about the sons of the prophets. On a certain occasion, when the sons of the prophets were cutting timber, it appears that the axe fell off the handle into the water, and it seemed there was a great disturbance in the feelings of the young prophets. Why, says one, Master, the axe was borrowed, and it seems there was quite an anxiety about the axe on account of its being borrowed property. I have thought that had the circumstance transpired in these days the expression would have been on this wise, "O, it is no matter, Master, the axe was borrowed." But in those days they had feelings in regard to their neighbors, and in consequence of this the power of God could be manifested for the purpose of raising the axe from the bottom of the water. Thus we see they had feelings of interest for the welfare of their neighbors and friends as well as for themselves. (1 March 1857, JD, 4:243.)

We have got to know that it is our business to learn to secure the peace and happiness of those that are around us, and never take a course to trample upon the feelings and rights of our neighbors. Let a man go and trample upon the rights of a brother, and how long would it take him to destroy that feeling of confidence that had heretofore existed between them? It will take a great while. This is what we have to place our eye upon; I feel it so; in all our thinking, in all our movements, and in our secret meditations, we want to let our minds reflect upon the interests of all around; and to consider that they have rights and privileges as well as ourselves; we ought to have this firmly established in our minds. (1 March 1857, JD, 4:245.)

Unity will turn people in our favor. And I will say to the Latter-day Saints—you may call it prophecy if you choose—that if this people will be united and will keep the commandments of God, God will turn the popular sentiment of this nation in our favor; the nation will feel disposed to bestow upon us favor instead of persecution and destruction. (5 October 1882, JD, 23:292-93.)

We must be one with each other. We have got to attend to our duties, make use of that intelligence which is given us, that we may be one with each other. The high priesthood have got to do this, every husband must do this, that he may be full of the Holy Ghost, that he may be the means of sanctifying his wife and his children, and that he may be an instrument in the hands of the

Lord of extending the kingdom of God, and of aiding in the accomplishment of His purposes. (4 January 1857, JD, 4:157.)

By building up our friends we build ourselves. Now an individual, in order to secure the highest and greatest blessings to himself, in order to secure the approbation of the Almighty, and in order to continually improve in the things pertaining to righteousness, he must do all things to the best advantage. Let him go to work and be willing to sacrifice for the benefit of his friends. If he wants to build himself up, the best principle he can do it upon is to build up his friends. (1 March 1857, JD, 4:243-44.)

Priesthood holders should learn to be one with their brethren. The high priests and seventies, they ought to be one with the Twelve Apostles, and they ought to learn to echo our sentiments as we echo those of the First Presidency, for we must all learn to be one. (4 January 1857, JD, 4:159.)

We can enjoy heaven on earth. Now if you want to get heaven within you, and to get into heaven, you want to pursue that course that angels do who are in heaven. If you want to know how you are to increase, I will tell you, it is by getting godliness within you.

Let angels be here, do you suppose that they would enjoy themselves here? They would until they felt disposed to leave. Well just so individuals can enjoy heaven around them in all places. We have got to go to work and do this; we must go to work and establish heaven upon this earth, notwithstanding the evils that are around us, the devils that are around us, and notwithstanding the wickedness that exists, still we have got to go to work and establish heaven upon this earth.

A person never can enjoy heaven until he learns how to get it, and to act upon its principles. (1 March 1857, JD, 4:246.)

CHAPTER 21

The Last Days

Faithfulness will prepare us for the Second Coming. If you are on a moving train of cars, as long as you sit still and occupy your seat that train will take you to the point you wish to go; but if you step off the cars it will be dangerous, and it may be a long time before another train will come along. It is the same with us—if we are living right, doing our work, we are going along, and if we are keeping our covenants, we are doing the work of God and accomplishing His purposes, and we will be prepared for the time when Jesus the Son of God will come in honor and glory, and will confer upon all those who prove faithful all the blessings that they anticipate, and a thousand times more. (18 April 1887, MS, 49:244.)

How many have their lamps trimmed? How many now here are ready—having oil in their vessels, and lamps trimmed, and prepared for coming events?

I am not sorry, nor do I regret on account of the near approach of these fiery ordeals. The Church, no doubt, needs purifying. We have hypocrites among us, milk-and-water Saints, those professing to be Saints, but doing nothing to render themselves worthy of membership; and too many of us have been pursuing worldly gains, rather than spiritual improvements, have not sought the things of God with that earnestness which becomes our profession. Trials and afflictions will cause our hearts to turn towards our Father who has so marvelously wrought out our redemption and deliverance from Babylon. (10 January 1886, JD, 26:367-68.)

The wicked will destroy themselves. Our object is the tempral salvation of the people as much as it is for their spiritual salvation. By and by the nations will be broken up on account of their wickedness. The Latter-day Saints are not going to move upon them with their little army; they will destroy themselves with their wickedness and immorality. They will contend and quarrel one with another, state after state and nation after nation, until they are broken up, and thousands, tens of thousands, and hundreds of thousands will undoubtedly come and seek protection at the hands of the servants of God, as much so as in the days of Joseph when he was called upon to lay a plan for the salvation of the house of Israel. (14 January 1872, JD, 14:309.)

A cloud is gathering in blackness. There is rapidly coming something that will try you, perhaps as you have never been tried before. All, however, that is necessary for us to do now is to see where our faults and weaknesses lie, if we have any. If we have been unfaithful in the past, let us renew our covenants with God and determine, by fasting and prayer, that we will get forgiveness of our sins that the Spirit of the Almighty may rest upon us, that peradventure we may escape those powerful temptations that are approaching. The cloud is gathering in blackness. Therefore, take warning. (6 May 1889, DW, 38:762-63.)

The last days will try men's hearts. The signs of the times, and the rapid approach of scenes that will try the hearts of the Latter-day Saints and their integrity, demand that we now seek earnestly the Spirit of God, and divine assistance, for it will certainly be needed in the scenes now rapidly approaching. We have needed it in the past. We can easily see that if we had not been in the possession of the Spirit of God to direct us through many of the scenes through which we have passed, we should not have been in the enjoyment of our present prospects of exaltation and glory, and our circumstances would have been much less favorable. And if we have needed the Holy Spirit in the past, we may truly understand that it will be needed in the future. (6 May 1889, DW, 38:762.)

The Saints will be preserved as Noah was. We should understand that the Lord has provided, when the days of trouble come upon the nations, a place for you and me, and we will be preserved as Noah was preserved: not in an ark, but we will be preserved by going into these principles of union by which we can accomplish the work of the Lord and surround ourselves with those things that will preserve us from the difficulties that are now coming upon the world, the judgments of the Lord. (5 October 1900, CR, pp. 4-5.)

The rulers of nations should prepare for the Lord's return. Awake, ye monarchs of the earth and rulers among nations, and gaze upon the scene wherein the early rays of the rising Millennial day gild the morn of the twentieth century! The power is in your hands to pave the way for the coming King of Kings, whose dominion will be over the earth. Disband your armies; turn your weapons of strife into implements of industry; take the yoke from the necks of the people; arbitrate your disputes; meet in royal congress, and plan for union instead of conquest, for the banishment of poverty, for the uplifting of the masses, and for the health, wealth, enlightenment, and happiness of all tribes and peoples and nations. Then shall the twentieth century be to you the glory of your lives and the lustre of your crown, and posterity shall sing your praises, while the Eternal One shall place you on high among the mighty. (1 January 1901, MFP, 3:334.)

The spirit of speculation will affect the Saints in the last days. I remember very clearly the troublous times which were experienced in Kirtland some fifty-three years ago. . . . At that time a spirit of speculation pervaded the minds of the people of this nation. There were money speculations, bank speculations, speculations in lands, speculations in city lots, speculations in numerous other directions. That spirit of speculation rose out of the world, and swept over the hearts of the Saints like a mighty wave or rushing torrent, and many fell, and apostatized. . . . Singular as it may appear, this spirit of speculation pervaded the Quorum of the Twelve Apostles and the Quorum of the Seven Presidents of Seventies; indeed, there was not a quorum in the Church but was more or less touched with this spirit of speculation. As that spirit increased, disunion followed. Brethren and sisters began to slander and quarrel one with the other, because their interests were not in harmony.

Will this be the case with the Latter-day Saints I am now addressing? I fear it is coming, but how far it will affect you it is not for me to say. (May 1889, DW, 38:767.)

The desert has blossomed. Yet here in this region of salt, alkali, and sagebrush, all but treeless and waterless, a region condemned by Webster, decried by Bridger, and shunned by the overland emigrant as a valley of desolation and death, Mormonism set up its standard and proceeded to work out its destiny. Beneath its touch—the touch of untiring industry, divinely blessed and directed—the desert blossomed, the wilderness became a fruitful field, and cities and towns sprang up by hundreds in the midst of the once barren waste. (2 January 1902, MS, 64:4.)

Nations shall be broken up. We have received revelation and, accordingly, we are here in these mountain valleys, and we are going to stay here. We shall cultivate our farms, and lay foundation for a time when the nations shall be broken up. Multitudes will then flee to these valleys of the mountains for safety, and we shall extend protection to them. You may say, shall you require them to be baptized and to become Latter-day Saints? Not by any means. If a gentleman comes into my neighborhood, a stranger, I will say, "Will you have something to eat? Is there anything I can do for you?" I am not anxious to make a "Mormon" of him, not by any means; we extend the hand of charity just as far as people are willing to allow us; but when, as I said at the beginning, people are crowding upon us, persons who are determined to destroy us and have not the principles of humanity in their bosoms, we cannot exercise that charity in their behalf that we desire. (14 January 1872, JD, 14:309.)

There will be a universal gathering to America and Palestine.
Mormonism teaches that prior to the Millennial reign of peace, there is to be a universal gathering of scattered Israel, the lineal descendants of Abraham, Isaac, and Jacob; meaning not only the Jews, but also the "lost tribes" and such of the chosen seed as have for generations been mixed with other peoples. This gathering, which includes the converted Gentiles, is preliminary to the glorious advent of the King of kings, and the resurrection of those who are Christ's at His coming. The places of assembly are America and Palestine, the former taking chronological precedence as the gathering place of "Ephraim and his fellows," while the "dispersed of Judah" will migrate to and rebuild Jerusalem. Here, upon the American continent, will be reared Zion, a new Jerusalem, where the Saints will eventually assemble and prepare for the coming of the Messiah. (2 January 1902, MS, 64:2.)

The Lord will not come until Jackson County is built up.
President Smith was talking yesterday about the land of Zion. Yes, surely, this entire continent is the land of Zion, and the time will come when there will be temples established over every portion of the land, and we will go into these temples and work for our kindred dead night and day, that the work of the Lord may be speedily accomplished, that Jesus may come and present the kingdom to His Father. He is coming soon, too. But we will not hear His voice until we build up Jackson County. Now we should make the preparation for this. We are not only going to have

Zion throughout this continent, but we will have it over the whole earth. (18 May 1899, MS, 61:546.)

Jesus will come. We ought to improve ourselves and move faster toward the point of perfection. It is said that we cannot be perfect. Jesus has commanded us to be perfect even as God, the Father, is perfect. It is our duty to try to be perfect, and it is our duty to improve each day, and look upon our course last week and do things better this week; do things better today than we did them yesterday, and go on and on from one degree of righteousness to another. Jesus will come by and by, and appear in our midst, as He appeared in the day when upon the earth among the Jews, and He will eat and drink with us and talk to us, and explain the mysteries of the kingdom, and tell us things that are not lawful to talk about now. (6 April 1898, CR, pp. 13-14.)

God will destroy the unrepentant. I say, in the name of Jesus Christ, the Holy Ghost having borne witness, that the anger of God is kindled against the abominations, hypocrisy, and wickedness of the religious world, and from the heavens has He uttered His voice in anger against those who "divine for money and teach for hire"; and unless they speedily repent, and be baptized for the remission of their sins, receiving the message the Almighty is now sending unto all people, they will be destroyed by the brightness of the coming of the Son of Man, which is now at hand—even at your doors—O ye inhabitants of the earth! (1841, SML, p. 87.)

CHAPTER 22

Tithing:
A Preparatory Law

Pay a full tithing. The time has now come for every Latter-day Saint, who calculates to be prepared for the future and to hold his feet strong upon a proper foundation, to do the will of the Lord and to pay his tithing in full. That is the word of the Lord to you, and it will be the word of the Lord to every settlement throughout the land of Zion. After I leave you and you get to thinking about this, you will see yourselves that the time has come when every man should stand up and pay his tithing in full. The Lord has blessed us and has had mercy upon us in the past; but there are times coming when the Lord requires us to stand up and do that which He has commanded and not leave it any longer. What I say to you in this stake of Zion I will say to every stake of Zion that has been organized. There is no man or woman that now hears what I am saying who will feel satisfied if he or she fails to pay a full tithing. (18 May 1899, MS, 61:533.)

Part of a tithing is no tithing at all. Now, I do not know how we can be justified in admitting people into our temples when they neglect this law of tithing. Of course, this has been done, and there have been hundreds, probably thousands, that have gone into our temples without paying one cent of tithing; and thousands have gone in there that have not paid a full tithing— and a part of a tithing is no tithing at all, no more than immersing only half a person's body is baptism. I do not know how bishops can justify themselves in giving recommends to such persons—they cannot after they hear what we have to say to them. When persons do not conform to the law to that extent that they can sanctify the land, and thus become unworthy to stand among the people of God, how can we be justified in conferring upon them the highest blessings that God ever bestowed upon man since the world began?

Brethren, I want you to think of these things; for the Lord has manifested to us most clearly that these things cannot go along in this way. It is now time for us to wake up, turn our attention to the Lord, and do our duty. (12 June 1899, JH, p. 13.)

Give a trifle more than is required. Another temptation is, How much money shall I give? That is a very strong temptation to most of us, I presume. Speaking of tithing as Brother Brigham has, how much of this tithing shall I give? Cannot I reserve a portion to myself? The Lord is very rich and I doubt if He will be troubled at all if I withhold a little for myself; and so a little to oneself is withheld. But that very little that is reserved will trouble that man, if his conscience is like the consciences of most of the Latter-day Saints. It will trouble him more or less in the day time, and also when he thinks of it at night. He does not have that happiness that it is his privilege to enjoy—it goes from him. One of the best things to do under such a temptation as that is to give, so as to be sure, a trifle more than is required. (9 April 1899, CR, p. 51.)

Never forget your tithing. God bless the Latter-day Saints. I want to have this principle so fixed upon our hearts that we shall never forget it. As I have said more than once, I know that the Lord will forgive the Latter-day Saints for their past negligence in paying tithing, if they will now repent and pay a conscientious tithing from this time on. But it would be woeful to think of the results if the Latter-day Saints had failed to listen to the voice of the servants of the Lord. It is God's truth that the time has now come when He will not look favorably upon our negligence of this principle. I plead with you in the name of the Lord, and I pray that every man, woman, and child who has means shall pay one-tenth of their income as a tithing. I beseech you to do this for the time has now come when the Lord is prepared to bestow upon us the choicest blessings. Our enemies are upon our path, and will if possible make us trouble. If we are unfaithful in this matter the same results will follow us as followed the people in Jackson County. (7 October 1899, CR, p. 28.)

The Lord will not protect those who neglect tithing. Through our nonobservance of this principle we have no promise but that we shall be driven from here as were the people in Jackson county. We cannot claim an inheritance in Zion, nor that the land has been sanctified as the Lord required. It is only through the wonderful mercies of the Lord that we have been protected and blessed with food, raiment, and shelter as we have been for many years past; it is not because we have proved ourselves worthy of these blessings by doing what the Lord has commanded. But now I tell you, in the name of the Lord, the time has come when it will not do for you and me to neglect our duties any longer in this respect. (12 June 1899, JH, p. 13.)

Teach children to pay tithing. Now, I have shaken hands with over eight hundred children, and I want to see those children grow up and become 80, 90, 100, or 140 years of age; and this will surely be the case if you will teach them these things that I am talking to you about today. Teach them to pay their tithing while they are young. You mothers, teach your children that when they get any money they should pay one-tenth of it to the Lord, however little it may be. Educate them to pay their tithing in full. Then we will have a people prepared to go to Jackson County. (18 May 1899, MS, 61:546.)

Tithing is a lower law. The law of tithing is a lower law, and was given of God. But the law of tithing does not forbid us obeying a higher law, the law of celestial union in earthly things. And the fact that we do not feel satisfied in simply obeying the law of tithing shows that it is a lesser law. Do you feel justified simply in obeying the law of tithing? Why, then, do you contribute to our temples and to bringing the people from the old countries, and to this object, and that, in thousands of ways, after you have properly and justly complied with the law of tithing? The fact that you do these things shows that you are not satisfied in merely obeying the law of tithing. In these contributions you are acting just as God designed you should act—by the light of the Holy Ghost that is in you. (19 October 1879, JD, 20:368.)

And so far as the law of tithing is concerned, there is about it something that is not of the same nature and character as the law of the united order. It was added because the people were not willing to comply with this noble and high celestial law, whereby they could act according to the light that is in them, and the power of the Almighty, by which they should be inspired. (19 October 1879, JD, 20:367.)

Tithe paying brings temporal and spiritual blessings. After the law of consecration was given, and the covenants entered into with the Lord by the people in Jackson County were broken, the Lord gave another law (tithing) six years later which was vastly different from the law of consecration. We are now under that law; and the same promises have been made to us if we will keep that law as were made to the people in Jackson County; the land will be sanctified, and we shall be counted worthy to receive the blessings of the Lord and to be sustained and supported in our financial affairs and in everything we do, temporal as well as spiritual. And it is a very small matter indeed, so far as sacrifice is concerned, in comparison to the giving of our entire property over to the bishop, and then receiving from him only a portion of it again as circumstances might demand. (12 June 1899, JH, p. 13.)

Tithing prepares us for the united order. Now, I will say in regard to the matter of tithing, I think that law was given to the Latter-day Saints, one object being to prepare them for and conduct them to the united order, that they might not fall into the same error as the people who were driven from the state of Missouri, but gradually be inducted into these higher principles. (21 April 1878, JD, 19:345.)

Tithing replaced the broken law of consecration. There was no one man in the Church that could have bought that land (Jackson County, Missouri); there were no two men, or half a dozen men, or a hundred men that could have bought it. The people as a general thing were poor. There were no rich men that received the gospel in those early days. But by combination and union they could have secured the means to carry out the purposes of the Almighty in regard to the purchase of that country. They failed because of their love for money. In a revelation after this we are told that they failed to give their names as they were commanded. The Lord sent elders throughout the states where there were Latter-day Saints, to collect means for this purpose; and the people in Jackson County were required to observe the law of consecration. But they failed to do it, and therefore the lands were not secured. The Lord could have sustained the people against the encroachments of their enemies had they placed themselves in a condition where He would have been justified in doing so. But inasmuch as they would not comply with His requirements, the Lord could not sustain them against their enemies. So it will be with us, or with any people whom the Lord calls to comply with His requirements and whom He proposes to confer the highest blessings upon, as He has in reference to us, and as He did in reference to the people in Jackson County.

There having been a failure in regard to this law of consecration—a failure so serious that it resulted in great misery to the people of God—a few years after that the Lord gave another law for the Saints to observe in place of the law of consecration. It is called the law of tithing. If we look upon this law in its proper light, we will see the importance of it and the danger that will result if we fail to observe it. (7 October 1899, CR, p. 24.)

The Saints must sanctify the land by paying tithing. The first principle of action to the Latter-day Saints is to sanctify the land by keeping this law of tithing and placing themselves in a position where they can receive the ordinances that pertain unto exaltation and glory of our dead. (7 October 1899, CR, p. 28.)

This law of tithing is one which, if it is not kept, the land shall not be sanctified unto those who disobey it, and it shall not be a land of Zion unto them. This is a plain and simple statement and can be understood by the most ignorant. Here we have been getting into debt to the Lord. (1 January 1901, MFP, 3:315.)

Our temporal salvation depends on our paying tithing. The poorest of the poor can pay tithing; the Lord requires it at our hands, to lay this matter plainly before the people, and we are going to do it. It is the temporal salvation of this Church, it depends upon obedience to this law. (August 1899, IE, 2:794.)

CHAPTER 23

Consecration and the United Order

The purpose of the united order is to unite and exalt the Saints. There are revealed, plainly and clearly, principles which are calculated to exalt the Latter-day Saints, and preserve them from much trouble and vexation; yet, through lack of perseverance on our part to learn and conform to them, we fail to receive the blessings that are connected with obedience to them. These principles of union, which the Latter-day Saints in former times ignored, and in consequence of disobedience to them were driven from Missouri, are called by different names—united order, order of Enoch, the principles of union of the celestial law, etc. When we search the revelations of God in regard to them, we see that wherever the gospel of the Son of God has been revealed in its fulness, the principles of the united order were made manifest, and required to be observed. The system of union, or the order of Enoch, which God has taken so much pains to reveal and make manifest, has been and is for the purpose of uniting the Latter-day Saints, the people of God, and preparing them for exaltation

---

Compiler's note:

The law of consecration and the united order, implemented in the 1830s and then discontinued, were given to the Prophet Joseph Smith as a part of the restoration of all things. While each Latter-day Saint certainly should strive to dedicate his time, talents, and means to the advancement of the kingdom of God consistently with authorized Church programs, any reinstitution of the law or establishment of a related organization would be improper unless done under the direction of the living prophet.

in His celestial kingdom; and also for the purpose of preparing them here on this earth to live together as brethren, that they may become one in all matters that pertain to their worldly affairs, as well as their spiritual interests; that they may become one—one in their efforts, one in their interests—so that there shall be no poor found in the midst of the Latter-day Saints, and no moneyed aristocracy in the midst of the people of God, but that there should be a union, an equality. (21 April 1878, JD, 19:342.)

The process of consecrating is liberal and generous. Now, this law, the united order, was given in 1831-32. Men were commanded consecration of property. Bishop Partridge, seeing there was some misunderstanding, wrote to Joseph for an explanation in regard to the matter. Joseph, in answer, says that in matters of consecration it should be left to the judgment of the consecrator how much he should give and how much retain for the support of his family, and not exclusively to the bishop; for, if so, it would give the bishop more power than a king possessed. There should be a mutual understanding between them, otherwise it should be left to a council of twelve high priests. Now where is the Latter-day Saint that cannot see a liberality, a generosity, in this matter, and be willing to submit to this tribunal? I would be willing to submit to the high council of this stake of Zion, or the high council of any other stake of Zion, and say, "Here is my property; say how much I ought to retain for my wives and children, and how much shall go into the common property of the Church." But I think my bishop and myself could settle the business at once. (19 October 1879, JD, 20:371.)

Lay all upon the altar. Let us go forth and do precisely as we are told; and just as fast as we increase, so will we have to use that spiritual knowledge which is given unto us in a way that will aid in building up the kingdom of God: and it is just so with what little property and means you have got; it must all be upon the altar. You must get rid of this little, mean, nasty spirit, and walk in the light of God. Let your minds expand, and be on hand for every duty that is placed upon you.

There are men right before me who have done but little for the kingdom of God, and who, if they knew what would be for their good, would go within twenty-four hours and say to President Young, "There is a thousand, or five or ten thousand dollars, which I will donate for the benefit of the kingdom. . . ." There are men who will do this at the present time; but by and by all the Saints of God will more generally learn the principle and obey it. (9 April 1857, JD, 5:66.)

Stewardships require giving our all. Now this law is very distinctly portrayed, and the Lord has made it so plain that He is determined that no man shall misunderstand Him. When He speaks He speaks in such a manner that there can be no dispute. He is not satisfied with telling it over once, He tells it the second and the third time; so that there can be no misunderstanding in regard to the mind of the Lord with reference to this law of a man's giving all, except that which is needed for his support, unto the Lord's storehouse. An observance of this law is what He says is required of every man in his stewardship. So that if the Latter-day Saints are appointed unto stewardships, or are satisfied to act as stewards before the Lord, this law is in force, and this law they should observe. I believe many do walk in the spirit of this law to a certain extent; and have complied with it, no doubt, in a manner in which they are justified before God; while some, perhaps, have paid no regard to it whatever. Some so far ignore these principles that they become very miserly and covetous. (19 October 1879, JD, 20:368.)

Parting with goods is a test. Take the man who has a large share of this world's goods, and examine what kind of a man he is; try his spirit, and you will generally find that it is often one of the greatest trials that can come upon him, to be called upon to part with any of his property. (9 April 1857, JD, 5:64.)

Consecration will prepare us for Zion. The law of consecration, which is in advance of the law of tithing, . . . is a principle which, as sure as I am speaking, you and I will one day have to conform to. When that day comes we will be prepared to go to Zion. (7 October 1900, CR, p. 62.)

Let every man seek the interest of his neighbor. Now a whole people, enlightened by the principles of high heaven in regard to these matters—filled with the Spirit of God, with the spirit of understanding, the spirit of philanthropy, every man seeking the interest of his neighbor, having an eye single to the glory of God, putting his means into the Lord's treasury, and no man saying that anything is his, except as a steward before God— would be a pillar of financial strength, a sublime picture of holy union and fraternity, and equal to the most extreme emergencies. Then when any misfortune befalls a man, such as the burning of his property, or failure or trouble in his department of business, he could go to the treasurer and say, "I have need of a certain amount to assist me in my stewardship. Have I not managed the affairs of my stewardship in a wise manner? Can you not have confidence in me? Have I ever misused the means put into my hands? Has it not been wisely controlled? If so, give me means to help me in my stewardship, or to build up this industry that is needed for the general interests of the whole." Well, it is to be given to him. There is confidence reposed in him because of his past conduct, and the course which he has pursued. He has due right in exercising his talents according to the light of the spirit that is within him. He understands fully the circumstances in which he is placed, and governs himself according to the obligations that rest upon him. He is found to be a wise, economical manager; and he is assisted in his stewardship to the extent of the means that he should have. (19 October 1879, JD, 20:370-71.)

Consecration is a celestial law. This persecution and expulsion [from Missouri] never would have occurred had the people observed the law which the Lord required. That law was simply the law of consecration—a law of the celestial kingdom. It was a law which, if observed, would have made the people the richest and wealthiest of any people in the world. There would not have been a poor Latter-day Saint in their midst. Every man would have had all he needed to make him happy and comfortable, so far as financial matters were concerned. But the law was rejected and the covenant broken; therefore the consequences came. (12 June 1899, JH, p. 13.)

Blessings come to those who obey the celestial law. I trust, my brethren, that we may devote ourselves entirely to the service of our God in the establishing of His Zion on the earth, zealously laboring in the interest of truth and righteousness on the earth, until it shall become a joy to us to be so engaged, that it may become second nature to us to serve God and keep His commandments, and to observe the celestial law, and that we may so enjoy the Holy Spirit in our hearts that we may overcome the world and establish the celestial law in our minds and establish it in our practice; that we may so understand ourselves and our privileges that we may in this life secure a considerable portion of the blessings that pertain to the celestial law, and which are to be enjoyed in the celestial glory; that so far as God gives us power in the earth, so far as He gives us possessions, houses and lands, flocks and herds, that these possessions shall become sanctified by our doings and actions. (8 April 1880, CR, p. 81.)

The Lord established the united order. The Lord, in Kirtland, established a united order. He called certain individuals, and united them by revelation, and told them how to proceed; and every man who would subscribe fully to the united order will proceed in the same manner. He told those people and the Church afar off to listen and hearken to what He required of men in this order, and of every man who belonged to the church of the living God—that all that they received above what was necessary for the support of their families was to be put in the Lord's storehouse, for the benefit of the whole Church. This is what is required of every man in his stewardship. And this is a law that is required to be observed by every man who belongs to the church of the living God. Now, this is one of the main features of the united order. We are not going to stop here, in these valleys of the mountains. Many of us expect to go forth and build up the center stake of Zion; but before we are called, we must understand these things, and conform to them more practically than many of us do at the present time. (21 April 1878, JD, 19:346.)

The united order is a celestial law. There is a widow, whose income is ten dollars; she pays one for tithing, and then has to appeal to the bishop for support. Here is a rich man who has an income of one hundred thousand dollars, and pays ten thousand for his tithing. There remains ninety thousand, and he does not need it, but the poor widow requires much more than she had before complying with the law of tithing.

Now what would be the operation of the celestial law? The widow has not enough for her support, therefore nothing is required of her by the celestial law, or the law of the united order. This rich man with his ninety thousand dollars, continues to increase his riches, pays his tithing fully, and yet wholly disregards the law of stewardship, or the law of temporal union. I cannot believe that a Latter-day Saint is justified in ignoring the higher law. (19 October 1879, JD, 20:369.)

The celestial law is to be lived voluntarily. We cannot be forced into living a celestial law; we must do this ourselves, of our own free will. And whatever we do in regard to the principles of the united order, we must do it because we desire to do it. Some of us are practising in the spirit of the united order, doing more than the law of tithing requires. We are not confined to the law of tithing. We have advanced to that point that we feel to soar above this law. (21 April 1878, JD, 19:346.)

The united order is no small thing. Before this church was organized, in April 1830, there were given revelations touching the united order; and from the day the first revelation was given in regard to these principles, there have been given a great number of revelations making the principle of the united order very plain to the understanding of those who wish to comprehend them. The principles and system have been pointed out in various revelations very distinctly, so that the Saints might not err. The Lord has shown us that He considered this order no small matter, but a subject of vast importance; so much so, in fact, that He has pronounced severe penalties on those who disobey its principles, and promised most important blessings to those who receive it and conform to its requirements. Doctrine and Covenants 78, 82, 85, 101. (21 April 1878, JD, 19:342.)

The united order is for spiritual and temporal unity. The purpose of the [united] order is to make the members of the Church equal and united in all things, spiritual and temporal; to banish pride, poverty, and iniquity; and introduce a condition of things that will prepare the pure in heart for the advent of the world's Redeemer. (2 January 1902, MS, 64:23.)

The united order requires godliness. "It doth not yet appear what we shall be, but we know that when he shall appear we shall be like him." This spirit should influence us in all our dealings. If we all acted in keeping with its sacred whisperings, there would be little difficulty in the establishment and working of the united order, for all would then be faithful in the performance of their several duties. (31 January 1877, DN, 25:834.)

The united order was not just for Missouri. Wherever there is a people of God, the principles of the united order are applicable, if they would receive and obey them. Some have thought that the united order was to be kept only by the people who should go up to the land of Missouri. Now this, I believe, is incorrect. (21 April 1878, JD, 19:343.)

The united order is like Noah's ark. We should understand that the Lord has provided, when the days of trouble come upon the nations, a place for you and me, and we will be preserved as Noah was preserved, not in an ark, but we will be preserved by going into these principles of union by which we can accomplish the work of the Lord and surround ourselves with those things that will preserve us from the difficulties that are now coming upon the world, the judgments of the Lord. (5 October 1900, CR, pp. 4-5.)

The united order must be based on righteousness. The principles of the united order . . . are sacred, and I assure you we will never go back to Jackson County, Missouri, there to build up the New Jerusalem of the latter days, until there is a perfect willingness on our part to conform to its rules and principles. Many years have transpired since we received the revelation of the united order, and in one sense that long period of time bespeaks negligence on our part in not more fully obeying it. The very principles of that order, in my estimation, were given for our temporal and spiritual salvation. In order to derive the benefit that God designed should flow from them, they must be established and systematized on the principle of righteousness, each person learning to love his neighbor as himself. For us to undertake to deal with them on any other principle would virtually open the way to bitter disappointment. (5 April 1877, JD, 18:375-76.)

Obedience would bring safety and union. Now, were the Saints all acting in the spirit of these revelations, what a happy community we would be! We would all be safe, and no man would need remain awake at night thinking what he should do for his family to keep them from begging their bread, or going to the bishop, which perhaps is only one degree better. And there would be a union that would be in accordance with the union of Enoch and his people, when they were taken to the world above —a union pleasing to the Almighty, and according to the principles of the the celestial world. (19 October 1879, JD, 20:371.)

CHAPTER 24

The Kingdom of God: A Stone Rolling Forth

We belong to the kingdom of God. As Latter-day Saints we know no nationality; we belong to the kingdom of God. As Paul said in his day: "By one Spirit are we all baptized into one body, whether we be Jews or Gentiles, whether we be bond or free." That Spirit has been bestowed upon us all, from whatever nation we may have come, and it has united us together and made us one people. Springing from many nations and speaking different languages, we have, under the influence of this Spirit become a homogeneous whole, dwelling together in peace and harmony. A really remarkable work has been accomplished in this direction, and no power but that of God could have done it. It should be a testimony to the world that God is with us; for this wonderful union of people of so many different nationalities cannot be accounted for in any other way. (16 August 1901, JH, p. 5.)

Seek the kingdom first. Now let me ask the question, Who does possess anything, who can really and truly call any of this world's goods his own? I do not presume to, I am merely a steward over a very little, and unto God I am held accountable for its use and disposition. The Latter-day Saints have received the law of the gospel through the revelations of God, and it is so plainly written that all can understand. And if we understood and comprehended the position we assumed in subscribing to it when we entered into its covenant through baptism for the remission of sins, we must still be conscious of the fact that that law requires us to seek first the kingdom of God, and that our time, talent and ability must be held subservient to its interest. If this were not so, how could we expect hereafter, when this earth shall have been made the dwelling place of God and His Son, to inherit eternal lives and to live and reign with Him? (31 January 1877, DN, 25:834.)

The Church is growing into manhood. Seventy years ago this Church was organized with six members. We commenced, so to speak, as an infant. We had our prejudices to combat. Our ignorance troubled us in regard to what the Lord intended to do and what He wanted us to do. Through the blessings of the Lord, however, we managed to move along in our stage of infancy, receiving support from the Lord as He saw proper to give it. We advanced into boyhood, and still we undoubtedly made some mistakes, which did not generally arise from a design to make them, but from a lack of experience. We understand very well, when we reflect back upon our own lives, that we did many foolish things when we were boys, because of our lack of experience and because we had not learned fully to obey the instructions of our fathers and mothers. We could not then comprehend that it was absolutely necessary, for our proper advancement, that we should observe the counsels of our parents. Many of us afterwards learned it, but too late perhaps to correct ourselves. Yet as we advanced, the experience of the past materially assisted us to avoid such mistakes as we had made in our boyhood.

It has been so with the Church. Our errors have generally arisen from a lack of comprehending what the Lord required us to do. But now we are pretty well along to manhood; we are seventy years of age, and one would imagine that after a man had lived through his infancy, through his boyhood, and on until he had arrived at the age of seventy years, he would be able, through his long experience, to do a great many things that seemed impossible and in fact were impossible for him to do in his boyhood state. When we examine ourselves, however, we discover that we are still not doing exactly as we ought to do, notwithstanding all our experience. We discern that there are things which we fail to do that the Lord expects us to perform, some of which He required us to do in our boyhood. But we feel thankful and grateful that we are enabled now, through our past experience, to accomplish many things that we could not do in former times and that we are able to escape individual sins that have brought trouble upon us in times past. While we congratulate ourselves in this direction, we certainly ought to feel that we have not yet arrived at perfection. There are many things for us to do yet. (6 April 1900, CR, pp. 1-2.)

The kingdom will never stand still. "Stand still, and see the salvation of the Lord." It appears from this verse which I will read that Moses began to cry unto the Lord for deliverance; and the Lord answered him saying: "Wherefore cryest thou unto me? Speak unto the children of Israel that they go forward." There was no standing still; there never has been since the day that the Almighty commenced to establish His work; the people have always been required to move on and never stand still. Although the Lord will work and accomplish wonders in regard to the deliverance of His people, when impediments arise in the path of their progress and no human power or ability can remove them, then God by His power will do so; but it is the business of those who profess to be engaged in His work to move on, to go forward, and that too without murmuring or having to be urged. So long as there remains a step forward to be taken, that step should be taken. . . . There is no standing still with the Latter-day Saints. When we were driven from Kirtland and Jackson County by mob violence, the purposes of God were being fulfilled and the work was undergoing changes necessary to its growth and progress, and the trials and afflictions incident thereto were necessary to the proving of the Saints and the establishment of the kingdom of God upon the earth. (7 April 1882, JD, 23:151-52.)

The purposes of God will be accomplished. We have no occasion for fear or cause for trembling: the purpose of God will be accomplished. What He has recommenced will be consummated though the combined armies of the earth should rise up and oppose. It is a fact that God has spoken, and called latter-day Israel from among the nations, and planted them in these valleys; therefore this work is His, and although He may lead us as He did Israel of old, into seemingly desperate situations, requiring serious sacrifices—the despoiling of homes, incarceration in prison, and even jeopardizing our very existence—and yet it will be but for a moment, as it were, and then those trials will terminate as did Job's, in an increase of possessions; and as ancient Israel's, in a kingdom and country, honor, glory, and dominion. (10 January 1886, JD, 26:367.)

God will deliver us. It is not in the economy of the Almighty to permit His people to be destroyed. If we will do right and keep His commandments, He will surely deliver us from every difficulty. (5 October 1882, JD, 23:293.)

The work must go on. Let the work of building temples and houses of worship go on; let Israel continue to educate their children and bring them up in the fear of the Lord, and let the gospel still be carried to the nations afar, and Israel be gathered and the people always be found moving on as the purposes of God continue to be fulfilled. Do not stand still and expect to see the salvation of God, but move on so long as there is a step to be made in the direction that He has commanded, and then see the salvation of the Almighty. This is the work of God, and He is directing its course and progress in the earth, and this work should ever be uppermost in our minds; and so long as we are found in the path of duty we can surely remain fixed and unmoved and determined in our purpose. (7 April 1882, JD, 23:152-53.)

The kingdom is a guide. Brethren and sisters, God has set up His church and kingdom on the earth for the benefit and blessing of the human family, to guide them in the way of truth, to prepare them for exaltation in His presence and for His glorious coming and kingdom on the earth. His purposes will be accomplished in spite of all the opposition which may be brought against them by wicked men and the powers of darkness. Everything that stands in the way of this work will be removed. Nothing will be able to withstand His power, but everything that He has decreed will be fully and perfectly accomplished. The love of God for His people will continue and abide and they will triumph in His might. (8 October 1898, DW, 57:513-14.)

The desert has blossomed as a rose. This gospel was preached, and thousands of Saints have been gathered from almost all parts of the globe, who are now scattered throughout the length and breadth of this Territory, making farms, building houses, planting orchards, and reclaiming the soil; creating villages, towns, and cities where nothing but wild beasts and savages used to roam, and causing the desert to blossom as the rose. Yet all this has not been accomplished by human wisdom, although the enemies of the Saints would try to make the world believe so; it has been done by the wisdom and power of Almighty God, whose outstretched arm has been over His Saints, preserving them from evil of every kind. (9 October 1869, JD, 13:254.)

The Church will stand. This Church will stand, because it is upon a firm basis. It is not from man; it is not from the study of the New Testament or the Old Testament; it is not the result of the learning that we received in colleges nor seminaries, but it has come directly from the Lord. The Lord has shown it to us by the revealing principle of the Holy Spirit of light and every man can receive this same spirit. (6 April 1900, CR, p. 3.)

Mormonism cannot be destroyed. Well, what have we to fear with regard to persecution and with regard to attempts that are made to destroy the principles of "Mormonism"? We know they cannot be destroyed. Our enemies, if permitted, may kill the President of our Church, they may kill his counselors and the Twelve Apostles, they may destroy the Seventies, and even the whole of the priesthood, but the principles of "Mormonism" they cannot destroy. The principles of "Mormonism" are eternal; they emanate from the God of heaven, and never can be destroyed. (5 October 1882, JD, 23:292.)

We will succeed against great odds. We talk about people succumbing because of their inferiority in numbers or because they are partly in the minority. That may be all very well providing it is simply man's work. We can very well see that in such case 150,000 could not expect to prosper or succeed in opposition, or in holding principles that are in conflict to those of 45,000,000 of people. Noah could not expect to succeed against a whole generation while his doctrine was accepted only by seven individuals, providing it had been only man's work. Neither could Moses when he proclaimed his message expect to have succeeded against the Egyptian government and its influence had he not been inspired and had authority from God. (6 October 1879, JD, 20:331.)

The world thinks we will be destroyed. The world thinks that the Latter-day Saints will be destroyed; they think that the Latter-day Saints will be scattered; they think that the time will come when the Latter-day Saints will be disunited and become like the sectarian world, and they have foolishly set to work to accomplish this purpose. Well now, as Brother Woodruff has said, we know better. We understand that this is the kingdom that was spoken of by Daniel the prophet, that should be set up in the last days, that should be no more thrown down nor given to another people. (5 October 1882, JD, 23:291-92.)

This is the work of the Almighty. Now talk about this kingdom being destroyed! Talk about, reason upon, lay plans here and there by the combined wisdom of governments to destroy the kingdom of God; why, you might as well try to pluck the stars from the firmament or the moon or the sun from its orbit! It can never be accomplished, for it is the work of the Almighty. I advise every man who has a disposition to put forth his hand against this work, to hold on and consider. Take the advice of Gamaliel the lawyer. Said he: "If this is the work of God, ye can do nothing against it; if it is not, it will come to naught." (14 January 1872, JD, 14:307.)

Nothing stops the work. The Apostles, notwithstanding the opportunities they had of acquainting themselves with the purposes of the Almighty, through personal converse with the Son of God, thought there was a time when they would have to stand still and cease their labors as ministers of God. When they saw the Savior hanging upon the cross in the agonies of death, their hearts failed them, and they concluded that all was over with them. They had thought that Jesus was to be king of Israel, and deliver them from the Gentile yoke, but now their hopes seemed vain and all was lost; now said their leader, Let us go a fishing. Was there a cessation of the work of God, when Jesus was suffering upon the cross? No, the work was still going on, but the Apostles did not understand it; they did not seem to comprehend the fact that the purposes of God were being carried out when He was suffering upon the cross. But when Jesus appeared to them after He arose from the tomb, He gave them to understand that in His suffering and death the words of the prophets were being fulfilled; and He opened their understanding that they might understand the scriptures. (7 April 1882, JD, 23:152.)

No power can prevent us. There is no power that can prevent us, as there has been none in the past. We have received too much knowledge to be thwarted in our purposes. Those who desire to persecute and overthrow Mormonism, let them go on and do their work; that is for them to do. Our work is to grow in the knowledge of God, to keep the commandments of God, to be faithful and to continue to increase and to become more and more perfect as we advance in years. (6 April 1900, CR, pp. 3-4.)

Thousands are fighting against us. There are thousands of people that are fighting against us who would, if they knew what we know, lay down their weapons and suppress the spirit to contend against us. The time will come when they will know it. It will not be in our day, but it will be in somebody's day here on the earth, or on some other earth. (7 October 1899, CR, p. 29.)

The Lord will frustrate the wicked. Let us continue, brethren and sisters, to work in the name of the Lord our God; gathering wisdom and intelligence day by day, that every circumstance which transpires may minister to our good and increase our faith and intelligence. If we continue to work righteousness, being faithful to each other and to God, no power will be able to overthrow us; and as brother Hyde remarked, for every stumbling block that our enemies place in our way, to hinder and prevent the work of God from moving forward, two will be placed in the paths of those who put one in ours. If we are faithful and keep the commandments of God, His works will continue to prosper until the prophecies are fulfilled, and we become a great, a glorious, and a mighty people. (9 October 1869, JD, 13:259.)

The Church does not fight its enemies. It is not our business to fight our enemies. There is no man or woman on the face of the earth, but is our brother or our sister. They are the children of God and we are here to bear and forbear with them in their interest and for the glory of God. It is not our business to destroy life. It is not our business to make war upon our enemies. They should let us alone. I would not say that I could govern and control my passions if a man were to try to take my life. That is another thing altogether. But it is not our business to fight them. They are our brethren and sisters and God have mercy upon them. That should be our prayer. (7 October 1899, CR, pp. 28-29.)

Our motto should be "The kingdom of God or nothing." May we be faithful in all of our labors, having the motto indelibly stamped upon our hearts, "The kingdom of God or nothing." (8 April 1880, CR, p. 82.)

The truth will prevail. No impediment placed in the way would ever prevent the onward progress of the Church of Christ. Dark clouds may sometimes pass over our heads, we may be sorely tried and perplexed, and efforts made to thwart us; but the truth is mighty and will prevail. (5 October 1889, JH, p. 5.)

Thus, in the short space of twenty years, a work has been accomplished without a parallel in the world's history. A work which has been tested on every side; it has been the object of misrepresentation in every part of the world; it has been opposed by the most talented theologians; it has overcome difficulties the most appalling; it has passed through trials the most fiery, and, like gold issuing from the furnace, has shone brighter and brighter; and while it has surmounted every obstacle, it has not only shown that "truth is mighty and will prevail," but has also shown that it has been sustained by One whose arm is omnipotent, and whose word shall be fulfilled and work accomplished though earth and hell oppose. (1851, BLS, p. 168.)

Zion—The Condition
and the Place

The Saints will not return to Jackson County until they are fully prepared. [President Snow read Doctrine and Covenants 105:2-10.] Hence we learn that the Saints in Jackson County and other localities refused to comply with the order of consecration, consequently they were allowed to be driven from their inheritances; and should not return until they were better prepared to keep the law of God, by being more perfectly taught in reference to their duties, and learn through experience the necessity of obedience. And I think we are not justified in anticipating the privilege of returning to build up the center stake of Zion until we shall have shown obedience to the law of consecration. One thing, however, is certain: we shall not be permitted to enter the land from whence we were expelled till our hearts are prepared to honor this law, and we become sanctified through the practice of the truth.

The Lord required that those lands in Missouri should be obtained, not by force, but by purchase, through the consecra-

---

Compiler's note:

While President Snow's ardent desire to see Zion is reflected in his many statements about the return to Jackson County, he knew that the Saints were not ready, and he indicated that in any case before one could go he must be called. The living prophet today gives similar counsel. Hence no one should take President Snow's comments out of context and act independently in this matter.

tions of the properties of the Saints; and the manner was pointed out how these consecrations should be made, but it was disregarded. (7 October 1873, JD, 16:276.)

Zion must be established. However great may be your poverty, how stupendous your difficulties, it matters little; the word has gone forth in your favor, and no opposing arm can stay its course. Zion must be established, her lands inhabited, her cities built, her temples reared, and her sons become mighty and powerful; that she may rise "fair as the moon, clear as the sun, and terrible as an army with banners." And all nations shall fear and tremble, and stand afar off in the day of her majesty. (1 December 1851, MS, 13:364; BLS, p. 196.)

Build up Zion, not Babylon. What did we come here for? We came to build up Zion, not to build up Babylon. The voice of the Almighty called us out from the midst of confusion, which is Babylon, to form a union and a lovely brotherhood, in which we should love one another as we love ourselves. When we depart from this purpose, the Spirit of God withdraws from us to the extent of that departure. But if we continue in the extent of those covenants which we made when we received the gospel, there is a corresponding increase of light and intelligence, and there is a powerful preparation for that which is to come. And because of our faithfulness and our adherence to the covenants we have made, the foundation upon which we stand becomes like the pillars of heaven—immovable. (6 May 1889, DW, 38:763.)

Stick to the ship of Zion. Stick to the ship of Zion. If boats come to the side showing beautiful colors and making wonderful promises, do not get on the ship to go to the shore on any other boat, but keep on the ship. If you are badly used by any of those that are on the ship, who have not got the proper spirit, remember the ship itself is all right. We should not allow our minds to become soured because of anything that the people on the ship may do to us; the ship is all right, and the officers are all right, and we will be right if we stick to the ship. I can assure you it will take you right into the land of glory. (3 April 1897, DW, 54:482.)

My greatest desire is to see Zion established. Then let us live the lives of Latter-day Saints, that we may first beget confidence in ourselves; then we shall begin to have confidence in each other, in God, and in His promises. A people in this condition of progress would know no failures; everything would prosper that they put their hands to; they would grow in faith and in good works. I tell you, in the name of the Lord God, that the time is coming when there will be no safety only in the principles of union, for therein lies the secret of our temporal and spiritual salvation. We have been enabled to establish settlements, towns, and villages, and we have been abundantly blessed with the necessaries and conveniences of life, notwithstanding we have been slow to hearken to and obey the commands of Jehovah. I would to God that every bishop and presiding officer would this day, in this holy temple, covenant and swear before Him, the Lord our God, that they would turn and serve Him with all their might, mind, and strength, and work in the interest of the people as they would for themselves. For my greatest desire is to see Zion established according to the revelations of God, to see her inhabitants industrious and self-sustaining, filled with wisdom and the power of God, that around us may be built a wall of defense, a protection against the mighty powers of Babylon; and while the disobedient of our Father's family are contending, and filling up their cup of iniquity, even to the brim, and thus preparing themselves for the burning, we who are the acknowledged children of the kingdom, being filled with the righteousness and knowledge of God, may be like the wise virgins, clothed in our wedding garments, and properly prepared for the coming of our Lord and Savior. (5 April 1877, JD, 18:376.)

Zion will spread and increase. Zion stands and prospers, and it will not be long before the enemy will melt away as before the morning sun. Zion will spread and increase until she holds dominion over all the nations of the earth. (7 October 1857, JD, 5:326.)

It is high time to establish Zion. Let us try to build up Zion. Zion is the pure in heart. Zion cannot be built up except on the principles of union required by the celestial law. It is high time for us to enter into these things. It is more pleasant and agreeable for the Latter-day Saints to enter into this work and build up Zion, than to build up ourselves and have this great competition which is destroying us. (21 April 1878, JD, 19:349.)

Keeping the commandments makes Zion. Make this a land of Zion in very deed by keeping the commandments of God thereon; and strive to teach your children in such a way, both by example and precept, that they will unhesitatingly follow in your footsteps and become as valiant for the truth as you have been. (16 August 1901, JH, p. 5.)

The priesthood is called to establish Zion. We are told that the priesthood is not called to work for money, but to establish Zion. What a lovely thing it would be if there was a Zion now, as in the days of Enoch, that there would be peace in our midst and no necessity for a man to contend and tread upon the toes of another to attain a better position, and advance himself ahead of his neighbor! And there should be no unjust competition in matters that belong to the Latter-day Saints. That which creates division among us pertaining to our temporal interests should not be. (21 April 1878, JD, 19:346-47.)

Establish Zion in your hearts. I do not know how soon we may be called to build up Jackson County; but I feel it is nearer at hand than Latter-day Saints generally believe. When you look upon Jackson County and its surroundings at the present time, it looks like an impossibility. There are perhaps thirty thousand people settled there, adjacent to the temple location, and they are doing business very extensively. Looking at it naturally, it would seem as if a favorable arrangement for us to go back there could never arise. But when the Lord sets about to accomplish His purposes, He finds it easy to make it effectual. It will be so in this. I can imagine several ways in which the road would be perfectly clear, and the people be very glad for the Latter-day Saints to go back to Jackson County. As I said yesterday, establish the principles of Zion in your hearts, and then you will be worthy to receive Zion outside. (18 May 1899, MS, 61:546.)

Zion will spread over the whole earth. President [Joseph F.] Smith was talking yesterday about the land of Zion. Yes, surely, this entire continent is the land of Zion, and the time will come when there will be temples established over every portion of the land, and we will go into these temples and work for our kindred dead night and day, that the work of the Lord may be speedily accomplished, that Jesus may come and present the kingdom to His Father. He is coming soon, too. But we will not hear His voice until we build up Jackson County. Now we should make the preparation for this. We are not only going to have Zion throughout this continent, but we will have it over the whole earth. (18 May 1899, MS, 61:546.)

The city of Zion will be built in Jackson County. The site for the city of Zion was pointed out by the Prophet Joseph Smith as Jackson County, Missouri, and there some of our people settled in 1831, but were subsequently driven from their homes. This event, while it delayed the building of the city, did not change the place of its location. The Latter-day Saints fully expect to return to Jackson County and "build up Zion." Their exodus to the Rocky Mountains and their sojourn in the stakes of Zion, as the places are called which they now inhabit, they regard as preparatory to that return, and as events that had to be in order to fulfill scripture, notably these words of Isaiah: "O Zion, that bringest good tidings, get thee up into the high mountain" [Isaiah 40:9]. "And it shall come to pass in the last days, that the mountain of the Lord's house shall be established in the top of the mountains, and shall be exalted above the hills; and all nations shall flow unto it" [Isaiah 2:2]. (2 January 1902, MS, 64:2.)

Preparation is needful for the return to Zion. By and by the Lord will have prepared the way for some to return to Jackson County, there to build up the center stake of Zion. How easily this work can be accomplished after we have learned to build up cities and temples here to His divine acceptance! Our present experience is a very needful one. Without it, we should be totally unfitted for the performance of such a work. We read that the temple which Solomon built was erected without the sound of a hammer being heard. There had been a previous preparation and an experience gained in some distant locality, and a proper training. The materials were accurately prepared elsewhere, and when brought together were ready for setting, each piece to its proper place. As knowledge and efficiency are obtained gradually, we may expect that the experience that we are getting now in learning how to build up cities in our present condition, conforming as near as possible to the holy order of God, is in order to prepare us by and by to return to Missouri, whence we were driven, and there build up cities and temples to the name of the Most High, upon which His glory will descend. (5 April 1877, JD, 18:374.)

Consecration will be required before the Saints can return. I will assure you, my brethren, that you and I will never be selected and called to go to Jackson County until it is evident that we are willing to abide that law [consecration]. It is a perfect law. Had the people in Jackson County observed it, it would have united them together, made them immensely rich, and they could have accomplished all that the Lord desired. (12 June 1899, JH, p. 13.)

More faith and devotion are required. Before we are prepared to return to Jackson County, to build up the center stake of Zion, I believe that a system or order of things will be introduced for our practice, requiring more faith and devotion than, I fear, some of us possess at the present moment. (7 October 1873, JD, 16:273.)

The Saints must be prepared to return to Jackson County. A grand preparation is coming. Do you suppose that the Lord would ever send you and me back to Jackson County until He could feel perfectly assured that we would do those things which the people of Jackson County failed to do for lack of experience and faith? (7 October 1900, CR, p. 62.)

Jackson County will be purchased by tithing. I remember one time hearing President [Orson] Hyde (I think it was) speaking in regard to our going back to Jackson County, and he said that inasmuch as they had abused the Saints and wrested from them some of their possessions, when we went back we would follow the same course toward them. After he had got through, President Young spoke upon this, and he said the Latter-day Saints never would get possession of that land by fighting and destroying life; but we would purchase the land, as the Lord has commanded in the first place. And I will tell you that that land never will be purchased, except it is purchased by the tithing of the Latter-day Saints and their consecrations; never worlds without end. . . . If you and I ever get any possession upon the land of Zion, it will be by purchase, not by force. This has been the will of the Lord from the beginning. (7 October 1899, CR, pp. 26, 23.)

Latter-day Saints will be selected to go to Jackson County. We are going back to Jackson County, Missouri, one of these days. Now if it was proper to wish it I would not care if it was tomorrow, if word should come for us to go back to Jackson County and build up a great city there. The day will come when Latter-day Saints will be selected—all may not be called at once, but those who are worthy will be called. There will be no poverty in that day. There will be plenty of food, clothing, and other necessaries of life; and the father who has a family, if called suddenly to depart this life, will know that his wife and children will be taken care of, that provision will be made for their sustenance and comfort. But this is the united order that we sometimes hear mentioned, but the time perhaps has not yet come to establish it. But the Latter-day Saints will never be satisfied with any other arrangement that might be proposed. The nations of the earth have for a long time been trying to establish some principle by which they can be financially sustained, united, and live in peace, but have not succeeded. But the Lord has revealed a principle clearly and definitely so that there will be no mistake about it. The system will bring financial union to the Latter-day Saints, and we will be satisfied with it as we are now with the principles of the gospel. It will suit us. It is something that is natural. And then you and I will have no trouble about our children's temporal welfare. This will take place, and whoever goes to Jackson County will meet with that sympathy and friendship that were not met with in early days, and because of the absence of which the people were allowed to be driven out. (6 April 1898, CR, p. 14.)

Be in readiness to build the city of Zion. Then let us practice honesty and diligence in our various callings, seeking unity and to cultivate the spirit of brotherhood financially as well as spiritually, that we may be in readiness, upon call, to go forth and build up the center stake of Zion and prepare a house in which to meet the Lord our Savior and Redeemer. (31 January 1877, DN, 25:834.)

A temple will be built in Jackson County. Let us all exercise faith for the Lord to open the way that we may go back to Jackson County. A short time ago something occurred in this connection that was a little extraordinary. Two men came here—good, honest men, as I have every reason to believe—and to our surprise they wanted to establish a union between the Latter-day Saints and the Josephites. We asked them to explain themselves. They said they had received a revelation that the time had now come to build a temple in Jackson County, and in order that this might be accomplished, they had felt it was their duty to go to the Josephites. They do not believe in the Josephites any more than we do; but they went there and had a conversation with the president and council of the Josephites. It was proposed that they send four of their elders, that we send four of our elders, and that the Hedrickites (to which body these two men belonged) have four of their elders, and that all these elders should meet on the land of Zion and see if they could not make some arrangement by which the temple could be built. Of course, we could see very well that there was no use trying in that direction; but they seemed to have faith that it could be effected. In part these men may have had a manifestation. I believe that they were about right on the point that the time had arrived to build a temple; at least, the time is arriving when that temple should be built; but it will not be built by that class of people. It will be built by the Latter-day Saints in connection with the Lamanites. (7 October 1900, CR, pp. 62-63.)

I can tell you what I think: Many of you will be living in Jackson County, and there you will be assisting in building the temple; and if you will not have seen the Lord Jesus at that time you may expect Him very soon, to see Him, to eat and drink with Him, to shake hands with Him and to invite Him to your houses as He was invited when He was here before. I am saying things to you now of which I know something of the truth of them. (15 June 1901, DN, p. 1.)

CHAPTER 26

A Personal Testimony and Various Counsel

The faithful share a knowledge of the truth. I had been a member of this Church but a short time when I obtained, by a divine manifestation, a clear, explicit, and tangible demonstration of the truth of this work. Thousands and tens of thousands of Latter-day Saints, men and women, in private life, can testify to the same experience; and though I may know many principles in regard to this doctrine, which in their limited experience they may not understand, yet in that one fact they are equal to me in knowledge, equal to the messengers who have administered to them this gospel. (6 March 1886, JD, 26:375.)

We should search the revelations more diligently. There are principles which are revealed for the good of the people of God, and clearly manifest in the revelations which have been given. But in consequence of not being more persevering and industrious, we neglect to receive the advantages which they are designed to confer, and we think, perhaps, that it is not necessary to exert ourselves to find out what God requires at our hands, or in other words, to search out the principles which God has revealed, upon which we can receive very important blessings. (21 April 1878, JD, 19:342.)

I have tried to submit completely to the Lord's will. I can assure you, brethren and sisters, that I had no ambition to assume the responsibility which now rests upon me. If I could have escaped it honorably I should never have been found in my present position. I have never asked for it, nor have I ever asked the assistance of any of my brethren that I might attain to this position; but the Lord revealed to me and to my brethren that this was His will, and I have no disposition to shirk any responsibility nor to decline to occupy any position that the Lord requires me to fill. I have tried to serve Him, to overcome the weaknesses of the flesh and to bring myself with every power and faculty of my nature into complete subservience to His will, so that I might eventually reach the highest glory which it is possible for man to attain. (8 October 1898, DW, 57:513.)

The humble and obedient will receive knowledge from God. I testify before this assembly, as I have testified before the people throughout the different states of the Union, and throughout England, Ireland, Scotland, Wales, Italy, Switzerland, and France, that God Almighty, through my obedience to the gospel of Jesus, has revealed to me, tangibly, that this is the work of God, that this is His kingdom which Daniel prophesied should be set up in the last days. I prophecy that any man who will be humble before the Lord, any man who will, with childlike simplicity, be baptized for the remission of his sins, shall receive the gift of the Holy Ghost, which shall lead him into all truth and show him things to come; he shall receive a knowledge from the Almighty that His kingdom has been established in these latter days, and that it shall never be thrown down or be left to another people. (14 January 1872, JD, 14:306-7.)

Killing for sport is wrong. In Adam-ondi-Ahman, while gradually recovering from the effects of a malignant fever which had detained me a fortnight in Far West, under the constant and skillful nursing of my sister Eliza, for some time I was unable to either do or read much. One day, to while away the slowly passing hours, I took my gun with the intention of indulging in a little amusement in hunting turkeys, with which that section of the country abounded. From boyhood I had been particularly, and I may say strangely, attached to a gun. Hunting in the forests of Ohio was a pastime that to me possessed the most fascinating attractions. It never occurred to my mind that it was wrong—that indulging in "what was sport to me was death to them;" that in shooting turkeys, squirrels, etc., I was taking life that I could not give; therefore I indulged in the murderous sport without the least compunction of conscience.

But at this time a change came over me. While moving slowly forward in pursuit of something to kill, my mind was arrested with the reflection on the nature of my pursuit—that of amusing myself by giving pain and death to harmless, innocent creatures that perhaps had as much right to life and enjoyment as myself. I realized that such indulgence was without any justification, and feeling condemned, I laid my gun on my shoulder, returned home, and from that time to this have felt no inclination for that murderous amusement. (BLS, pp. 27-28.)

God will accomplish His work. As a servant of God I bear witness to the revelation of His will in the nineteenth century. It came by His own voice from the heavens, by the personal manifestation of His Son and by the ministration of holy angels. He commands all people everywhere to repent, to turn from their evil ways and unrighteous desires, to be baptized for the remission of their sins, that they may receive the Holy Ghost and come into communion with Him. He has commenced the work of redemption spoken by all the holy prophets, sages, and seers of all the ages and all the races of mankind. He will assuredly accomplish His work, and the twentieth century will mark its advancement towards the great consummation. (1 January 1901, MFP, 3:334-35.)

We possess the fulness of the gospel. We, the Latter-day Saints, profess to have received from God the fulness of the everlasting gospel; we profess to be in possession of the holy priesthood—the delegated authority of God to man, by virtue of which we administer in its ordinances acceptably to Him; and we testify to the whole world that we know, by divine revelation, even through the manifestations of the Holy Ghost, that Jesus is the Christ, the Son of the living God, and that He revealed Himself to Joseph Smith as personally as He did to His Apostles anciently, after He arose from the tomb, and that He made known unto him these heavenly truths by which alone mankind can be saved. (31 January 1877, DN, 25:834.)

We need to examine ourselves. It would be well to examine ourselves, hold communion with ourselves in the secret closet, to ascertain how we stand as elders in Israel before the Lord, so that if need be we may renew our diligence and faithfulness, and increase our good works. (6 May 1882, JD, 23:193-94.)

The Saints have advanced. We can look back now and we can see that we have advanced. We have not stood still, but we have been moving along and gradually increasing our growth. The child grows from childhood to boyhood, and from boyhood to manhood, with a constant and steady growth; but he cannot tell how or when the growth occurs. He does not realize that he is growing; but by observing the laws of health and being prudent in his course he eventually arrives at manhood. So in reference to ourselves as Latter-day Saints. We grow and increase. We are not aware of it at the moment; but after a year or so we discover that we are, so to speak, away up the hill, nearing the mountain top. (6 April 1899, CR, p. 2.)

Nothing should deter us from making our exaltation sure. Our prospects are sufficiently grand and glorious to cause us to put forth every exertion that we possibly can, in order to secure the blessings that are before us. Nothing should deter us from the exercise of every power that God has bestowed upon us, to make our salvation and exaltation sure. (6 October 1899, CR, p. 2.)

We do not berate others. Mormonism is pursuing its traditional policy: "minding its own business" and doing unto others as it would be done by. It does not spend its time berating and abusing other churches and religions, all of which it recognizes as doing good in their various spheres. It simply proclaims itself as a greater measure of truth as the fulness of the everlasting gospel: facing fearlessly all creeds, all systems, and inviting comparison between its doctrines and theirs. (2 January 1902, MS, 64:23.)

Example teaches better than words. Though one teach with the eloquence of an angel, yet one's good practices, good examples, one's acts, constantly manifesting whole-heartedness for the interests of the people, teach much more eloquently, much more effectually. (1 December 1851, MS, 13:362; BLS, p. 193.)

The earth will be translated. The whole earth is the Lord's. The time will come when it will be translated and be filled with the Spirit and power of God. The atmosphere around it will be the Spirit of the Almighty. We will breathe that Spirit instead of the atmosphere that we now breathe. (18 May 1899, MS, 61:546.)

We have a mother in heaven. We are the offspring of God. He is our Father, and we have a Mother in the other life as well. (9 October 1898, CR, p. 56.)

The Lord raised up reformers. We can trace the providences of the Almighty in raising up certain individuals to establish religious organizations, and we see in these things the workings of the Spirit of God for the general interest of the human family. (14 January 1872, JD, 14:304.)

America's founders were inspired. We look upon George Washington, the father of our country, as an inspired instrument of the Almighty; we can see the all-inspiring Spirit operating upon him. And upon his co-workers in resisting oppression, and in establishing the thirteen colonies as a confederacy; and then again the workings of the same Spirit upon those men who established the Constitution of the United States. In a revelation contained in the Doctrine and Covenants the Lord says: "And for this purpose have I established the Constitution of this land by the hands of wise men, whom I raised up unto this very purpose." We see the hand of the Lord in these things. (14 January 1872, JD, 14:304.)

The Lord framed the American Constitution. We trace the hand of the Almighty in framing the constitution of our land, and believe that the Lord raised up men purposely for the accomplishment of this object, raised them up and inspired them to frame the Constitution of the United States. (14 January 1872, JD, 14:301.)

The Manifesto came from God. When we were placed in certain circumstances with our wives and children, and the nation was pursuing us with the intention of destroying us, the Lord opened our way in a manner that we never expected. Very few indeed thought our deliverance would come in the way which the Lord saw proper to bring it. A sacrifice had to be made—a greater one than had ever been made before. The Church itself depended upon the Saints acting in a wise and prudent manner, and making the sacrifice that was required at that time. The word of the Lord came to President Woodruff. When that Manifesto was issued, you knew what it meant. Some were alarmed. They thought the Church would go to pieces; thought they were breaking their covenants; thought the Lord had withdrawn from them. But that Manifesto was issued by the command of the Lord; and the Saints humbled themselves before the Lord and bowed to the requirement. The heavens rejoiced and God smiled upon us. He blessed His people, and delivered us from our enemies, and they were brought to shame and disgrace. They thought to destroy the Latter-day Saints, but they failed in their attempt. Nevertheless, we had to make the sacrifice, and it was right that we should. The Lord could have delivered us in some other way, had He so wished; but He knew best, and that was the course He required us to pursue and the sacrifice He desired us to make. We made it, and He has blessed us wonderfully from that time to the present.

He has given us power among the nations, and in various ways the people have been raised in the estimation of the world. Men of great wisdom have looked upon us, though they may have been silent, and they have honored the course we have taken. The Lord required that of us. (18 May 1899, MS, 61:532.)

Let us try to be better. Let us decree in our hearts, let us inwardly testify to the Lord, that we will be a better people, a more united people at our next conference than we are today. This should be the feeling and determination of every man and woman present in this solemn assembly. I feel in my heart that I will try to be more devoted than I have been in the past to the interests of the kingdom of God and the carrying out of His purposes. (9 October 1898, CR, p. 55.)

God has revealed Himself to me. There is no man that knows the truth of this work more than I do. I know it fully; I know it distinctly. I know there is a God just as well as any man knows it, because God has revealed Himself to me. I know it positively. I shall never forget the manifestations of the Lord; I never will forget them as long as memory endures. It is in me. (5 October 1897, CR, p. 32.)

I have received a perfect testimony. I have been engaged in promulgating the principles of the gospel for the past fifty years, and I have received for myself a perfect testimony that this is the power of God unto salvation. (18 April 1887, MS, 49:241.)

I am one that has received from the Lord the strongest revelation concerning the truth of this work. That manifestation was with me powerfully for hours and hours; and whatever circumstances may occur in my life, as long as memory lasts this perfect knowledge will remain with me. (7 October 1900, CR, p. 61.)

The Spirit of God enveloped my whole system. Elder Sherwood, at that time one of the right hand men of the Prophet's, said to me, "Brother Snow, have you received the Holy Ghost since you were baptized?'' That question struck me almost with consternation. The fact was, while I had received all I needed perhaps, I had not received that which I had anticipated; and after Brother Sherwood put this question to me I felt dissatisfied, not with what I had done, but with myself. With that feeling I retired in the evening to a place where I had been accustomed to offer my devotions to the Lord. I knelt down under the shade of a tree, and immediately I heard a noise over my head like the rustle of silken garments, and there descended upon me the Spirit and power of God. That will never be erased from my memory as long as memory endures. It came upon me and enveloped my whole system, and I received a perfect knowledge that there was a God, that Jesus, who died upon Calvary, was His Son, and that Joseph the Prophet had received the authority which he professed to have. The satisfaction and the glory of that manifestation no language can express! I returned to my lodgings. I could now testify to the whole world that I knew, by positive knowledge, that the gospel of the Son of God had been restored, and that Joseph was a prophet of God, authorized to speak in His name, just as Noah was in his day. (20 July 1901, JH, p. 3.)

My testimony was revealed from heaven. Having become convinced by reasoning, and by listening to the testimony of others who had received these principles, I became satisfied that it was my duty to experiment upon these principles, that I might be able to test the results. This I consequently did, and there followed the same testimony and the same experiences, so far as the knowledge of the divinity of these principles was concerned, as followed obedience to this gospel as proclaimed by the Apostles in former times. And this knowledge could not be disputed. It was not only acknowledged intellectually, but the inspiration of the Holy Ghost imparted to me a knowledge as physical and as demonstrative as that physical ordinance when I was immersed in the waters of baptism; . . . as I had passed through the atmosphere into the element of water, so my experience, knowledge, and testimony were full and complete—so complete, indeed, that from that day till the present moment, through all of the vicissitudes of life through which I have passed, I have no more doubted the truth of these principles than I do now that I behold this audience, and I never can doubt it. As long as memory continues and reason shall assert its throne, I never can permit the powerful testimony and knowledge that was communicated to me to remain silent. It was revealed to me. The heavens were opened over my head, and the power of God and the light of the Holy Ghost descended and elevated my whole being, and gave me the most perfect knowledge that Jesus was the Son of God. It was not the result simply of opinion or belief, as is the case in many other things, but it was a knowledge far beyond that of belief or opinion. I knew that God had sent His angels and restored the fulness of the gospel as taught in ancient times; that He sent angels to authorize Joseph Smith, and gave him authority to administer in the ordinances of the gospel, and to promise the Holy Ghost to all who would be obedient. (18 April 1887, MS, 49:242.)

Index

Dependence, of man on God, 11
  on Spirit, 109
Desert, blossoming of, 152, 173
Desires, righteous, 60-61
Determination, trials overcome by, 33-34
  to do God's will, 43-44
Devotion, 43, 102
Diligence, 48
Disagreeableness, 61-62
Discouragement, 35-36
Dispensation of the fulness of times, 57
Disrespectfulness, 133
Divorce, 141
Duties, performance, 45-46
  taught by Spirit, 113

— E —

Earth, translation, 191
Earth life, preparation for exaltation, 94
  school of suffering, 119
  selected, 92
  See also Mortality
Education, of the Spirit, 114
Elders, happiness dependent upon, 79
Elijah, 36
Enduring to the end, 127
Enemies of the Church, 19, 176
Enjoyment, capacities for, 60-61
Enoch, 36
Entrepreneurs, 63
Envy, 131
Esther, 116
Eternal family, audience before, 99-100
  endless reign, 138
  governance, 3
Eternal increase, 3
Eternal laws, perfection produced by, 37
Exaltation, earth life preparation for, 94
  families should seek, 138
  man's opportunity, 100
  priesthood channel for, 75, 78
  sureness of, 190
Example, followed by children, 134
  teaching by, 78-79, 191
Experience, 24, 30

— F —

Faith, severe trials bring, 121
  Spirit brings, 113
Family, fathers should instruct, 135
  progress, 136-37

Family unity, 132-34, 136
Farmers, 46
Fathers, counsel of, 46, 134
  instruction of children, 134-35
  must possess Spirit, 133
  perfection, 132
  sensitive, 135
  sustaining, 136-37
Fault-finding, 61
Faults, correction of, 133
Feelings, consideration of, 146-47
  hurt, 179-80
Fellowship, members unfit for, 103
Fidelity, to be sought ambitiously, 79
"Fiery furnace," 44
Finance, personal, 131, 185
First estate. *See* Premortal life
First principles of the gospel, 25
"Following the Brethren." *See* Priest-
  hood leaders
Folly, 33, 35
Founding Fathers, 191-92
Free agency. *See* Agency
Friends, 148
Friendshipping, 153
Friendships, missionary work brings, 70
Fulness of the Father, 28, 32
Fulness of the gospel, 189-90
Fulness of the priesthood, 79

— G —

Gathering of Israel, 153
Gathering to Zion, 32
General Conference, 89-90, 112
Gift of the Holy Ghost, leads to truth,
  106
  principle of revelation, 107
Gloominess, antidote for, 61
Glory of God, singleness to, 11, 47,
  107-8
God, unity required for seeing, 145-46
  communication, 10
  desires universal salvation, 91
  glorified by our overcoming trials, 126
  hand manifest in world, 13
  helps overcome trials, 123-24
  knowledge from, 26-27
  love of man, 14
  made our first parents' clothes, 76
  manifestations, 193-95
  progression, 3
  promises, 3, 12